Be Happy... Feel Great!

Change Your Habits Change Your Life

Michael Malkush

Be Happy…Feel Great! Copyright © 2014. All rights reserved. No part of this book can be reproduced in any manner, without written permission from the author, except brief quotations in critical articles or reviews.

To order in bulk, contact the author at www. BeHappyFeelGreat.com

© Copyright 2014, Michael Malkush
All rights reserved.

Disclaimer

The information provided in this book is designed to provide helpful information on the subjects discussed. This book is not meant to be used, nor should it be used, to diagnose or treat any medical or psychiatric condition. For diagnosis or treatment of any medical or psychiatric problem, consult your own physician.

The publisher and author are not responsible for any specific medical or health needs that may require supervision by a licensed healthcare practitioner, and thus they are not liable for any consequences from any recommendation, to any person reading or following the information in this book.

Neither the publisher nor the author shall be liable for any loss of profit or any other commercial damages, including but not limited to special, incidental, consequential, or other damages.

Michael Malkush
PO Box 284
Cutchogue, NY 11935
www. BeHappyFeelGreat.com

Michael Malkush's new book "Be Happy…Feel Great!" is full of practical advice and ways of being that the reader can implement for immediate results. He clearly teaches principals that will help improve the reader's lives and sets up ways for the reader to be successful in following through to get the results. He gives clear examples and offers easy to follow systems.

Michelle DeBerge
Professional Life Coach, Motivational Speaker, Best Selling Author
Co-Founder of The CanDoBe Company

"Be Happy…Feel Great!" is a fun and helpful book to read, especially after a stressful day. It can help re-charge oneself to wake up to a new and better day. Each time I read it I find an idea that resonates with me to feel better about myself and enjoy each challenge. Michael offers systems to implement what you read in each chapter. The worksheets provide the support to apply the information and take action. I have and will continue to recommend this book to my co-workers and associates.

Ed Clearwater – Systems Operations
IBM Corp.

Michael Malkush masterfully creates a useful and practical book that coaches can recommend to their clients. "Be Happy…Feel Great!" has practical information and activity sheets at the end of each chapter to get the reader to apply what they read. His stories and anecdotes make a great book exceptional. You will certainly get a lot of life changing inspirations from reading this book. It's an easy to read format and the information it provides will appeal to a very broad audience. It is an awesome follow-up to, "Nothing Good Comes from a BUT."

Christopher Michael
Addiction Recovery Coach

Foreword

As a marketing and publishing consultant I am constantly reading self-development materials in service to my clients. So when "life transformation" specialist Michael Malkush asked me to write the foreword to his book I was greatly honored, and thought long and hard about what to say. My challenge was that I didn't believe it WAS a book! As a consultant who frequently feels like a life coach, and has worked on so many best-selling books; I knew the program Michael was developing was so much more!

The **"Be Happy… Feel Great!" project** is the start to something wonderful for you. It's a treasure map that Michael has developed after a lifetime of mentoring others. It's an introduction to an interactive system he has created to help you know the happy, healthy life you not only seek, but have earned and deserve to be living. In this second book in his series of how-to guides for happy living, Michael shares on a more personal level from his deeper understanding of the human spirit, from his own experience of extreme trauma and the domino effect that had on his entire family.

You'll learn from a man who has conquered his own grief, from the worst personal tragedy and then given his life to nurturing others. Now those who are lucky enough to find out about him and practice what he teaches can experience the success of living fulfilling lives full of purpose and joy.

Anyone who has had to overcome hardship knows that success is being able to get up more times than life knocks you down. But how do we develop the strength of will and resilience to see us through?

In this book you will learn the fundamentals, and how to lay strong foundations on which to build. You'll learn effective habits, how to live life responsibly and responsively, taking care of the source of your health and joy, the true importance of wealth and timing.

This book is an engaging and easy read, but don't be fooled! The content is profound and timeless, and Michael has proven that it works. You will want to keep it handy and read it more than once. You might even grab some extra copies because you will likely find yourself wanting to lend it to the people you care about and love.

You can be happy and feel great, and you'll thank Michael Malkush for working so hard on this roadmap to help you get there, and how to get back when you lose your way.

Cydney O'Sullivan
Founder, The Millionaires Academy and Experts Success
9 Times Best Selling Author, mother, daughter, aunt, entrepreneur and joy seeker

Acknowledgements

First I would like to thank everyone who read my first book, *Nothing Good Comes from a BUT*. Your feedback, encouragement, and suggestions made me realize many of you wanted to dig deeper into your own personnel development and encouraged me to write a follow-up book.

Thank you to Cydney O'Sullivan, my writing coach and mentor who helped me every step of the way. She provided me with her team of experts with "Bestseller Success" to write, publish and help market this book.

I want to thank everyone at LTV Studios, especially Mike Tremblay and Lena Trbojevic who helped me to produce a very special television show, "Be Happy Feel Great." Also to the many guests that have appeared on the show, from which I have learned so much about personal transformation.

Thank you to Raphael Love, who helped me to develop my own social media platform in conjunction with my TV show and both of my books. Raphael has been very patient and is an excellent teacher who has been able to train and coach me throughout the process. His encouragement helped me to write this book.

Mike Boyd and Lubie Lubinsky who have advised and helped throughout the entire process of writing *Be Happy…Feel Great!*

Dave Herbert a former colleague of mine, at Jericho High School, who inspired me in so many ways to someday write a book.

Most of all I want to thank my family for all the love, energy and support they have given me throughout the entire writing process of *Be Happy Feel Great*. My wife Carol was very patient and did a great job reading and editing each segment. My children Chris and Missy offered their input and suggestions to make this book a better read. My grandchildren Jacob and Tyler, who continue to inspire me and teach me more about life every day.

This book is in memory of my sister Michelle Becker who I write about in my introduction and feel is always with me. From her I have acquired the strength and confidence to accomplish extraordinary things in my amazing life!

Table of Contents

I. INTRODUCTION 11

II. BE HAPPY, FEEL GREAT 17

    Chapter 1:   Forming Effective Habits 19

    Chapter 2:   Living The Responsible Life 29

    Chapter 3:   Well-Being – Taking Care Of The Source 37

    Chapter 4:   It's All In Your Head 61

    Chapter 5:   Be Here Now 73

    Chapter 6:   It's Always (And Never) About The Money 83

    Chapter 7:   Timing Is Everything 95

    Chapter 8:   Just Between You And Me… 103

    Chapter 9:   Are We There Yet? 109

    Chapter 10: Follow Your Dreams 117

III. Conclusion 127

I. INTRODUCTION

One day when I was teaching, the secretary came into my classroom to tell me that there had been a family tragedy and I had to leave immediately. The school received a phone call that my brother-in-law had drowned. My help was needed at my sister, Michelle's house. When I arrived, there were a lot of people inside and outside the house including; police, news reporters, friends and neighbors. Expecting to see my sister, I was told by a detective that she was missing and they suspected she had also drowned. Their children (ages 8, 13, and 16) were taken out of school and were safe with a family friend. "What happened?" I asked over and over again. Several scenarios were told to me, but none made sense.

I was brought down to where Bill's body was found earlier that morning. They told me he was found in his law enforcement uniform, between a boat and the dock. He and my sister were last seen alive supposedly around 10:30 pm the night before. Why wasn't the area where he was found roped off to investigate it properly? Why was everyone so sure my sister would be found dead in the water too? A double drowning at night, in a dark marina, was very suspicious to me. Instead the chief of police immediately claimed it was an accident.

I had to tell my parents what happened and bring them out. Other relatives arrived. The next afternoon a police detective came to the front door, to tell us that divers just found my sister's body. **I KNEW MY LIFE WOULD NEVER BE THE SAME…**

While funeral arrangements were being made, my wife and I hired a private investigator. His findings made this case more suspicious every day. My mother moved in to care for the children. My father came out on weekends. I left my teaching position and got a job to be closer to them. I took care of the legal affairs and oversaw my sister's business. I also had my own family, a wife and our 18 month old son to care for.

Today the children are all doing very well. They each received a good education and have good careers, friends and families. This is still an open case and even though I can never bring them back, I hope to find out some day what really happened.

From this terrible tragedy I personally gained an inner power and strength that I did not know I had. I realized that we are all fragile and how short life is. I learned how important family and good friends really are. I realized I could do anything that I set my mind to. On a spiritual level I felt guided by the loved ones I lost. My life has changed drastically since that day. I believe I have since been on a journey of helping people to appreciate what they have, enjoy each day and live their lives to the fullest.

In 2013, I published a book: *Nothing Good Comes from a But,* which quickly became an Amazon Bestseller. The purpose of that book was to highlight the excuses that people make in all areas of their life – relationships, careers, money, etc. – that stop them from achieving the happiness and success that they want in their lives. *Nothing Good* was written to assist readers in becoming aware of all the places where "But" was getting in the way of happiness.

Be Happy...Feel Great! is directed towards people who are ready to move beyond the "BUT" stage – they are ready to let go of their excuses and put their lives into action. Specifically, this book focuses on 10 areas – Habits, Responsibility, Well-Being, Mindfulness, Presence, Money, Time, Relationships, Growth and Dreams - and provides suggested structures and practices that you can use to support you as you create the life that you want.

If you are really serious about making changes in your life I recommend an accountability partner or hiring a coach to support you in implementing these practices, and taking them further than you are likely to take them on your own. The role of a coach is to bring out and help people discover their greatness and follow their passion. Coaching focuses on the positive attributes of the individual rather than negative emotions or correcting what is "wrong" with you or your life. Effective coaching is based on achievement, not therapy. A coach focuses on goals, dreams, and helps transform a life of emptiness to a life of fulfillment and happiness. Extraordinary results are made possible, and impossible dreams become a reality.

The tools described in this book are only a fraction of what I can offer to my coaching clients. While this book can certainly be used on its own, the suggested practices and structures take on a whole new level if combined with the support of a coach, and the resources available at www.behappyfeelgreat.com

What does it mean to Be Happy and Feel Great? The *Be Happy Feel Great* manifesto on the following page says it all. We created this for people to not only to feel great about their lives *right now*, but also to have the strength and courage to follow their dreams and passions regardless of the obstacles and circumstances. You can post the manifesto in your office at home and work, use it as the screensaver on your computer or tablet. You may also order a full-sized poster of the manifesto Be Happy Feel Great from the website above.

You have taken the first step by picking up this book. You wouldn't have done that if you didn't see that more was available in your life. You are right: there is more available. I believe that you have something to offer this world that only you can offer. I believe that you have everything you need, right now, to live the life of your dreams. You are ready to Be Happy and Feel Great.

Let's get started.

You can do ANYTHING You want

LIFE is short ENJOY it
you are very special Start doing things YOU LIKE to do
you deserve to FEEL GOOD & BE HAPPY
do it NOW, not LATER or TOMORROW HELP SOMEONE
Follow YOUR PASSION THIS IS YOUR LIFE if you want something, ASK FOR IT
think BIG say NO if you DON'T WANT TO DO SOMETHING
MAKE A DIFFERENCE REMEMBER what is LEARN SOMETHING NEW EVERY DAY
Exercise STOP WORRYING, It's a WASTE of energy
APPRECIATE WHAT YOU HAVE If you don't like something change it
Take ACTION NOW, follow YOUR DREAMS
STOP BLAMING and COMPLAINING do things YOU love GET RID of the CLUTTER in your life
put only GOOD things in YOUR BODY let's grows out ENJOY THE RIDE LOVE YOURSELF
surround yourself with POSITIVE people ALL things will eventually pass
TAKE RESPONSIBILITY, DON'T BLAME OTHERS Travel SEE THE WORLD
Don't dwell on the past, IT'S OVER AVOID those who bring you down
SMILE A LOT ☺ Each day is a NEW BEGINNING
you're not going that way
Go for a hike enjoy the beauty you see
THERE IS ALWAYS A WAY
Life is BETTER when you are LAUGHING

The "Be Happy Feel Great" Manifesto

Michael Malkush © 2013   www.behappyfeelgreat.com

II: BE HAPPY, FEEL GREAT

CHAPTER 1
Forming Effective Habits

"We are what we repeatedly do. Excellence is not an act then, but a habit."

- Aristotle

A habit is a recurrent, often unconscious pattern of behavior that is acquired by frequent repetition. Brushing your teeth before bed, making your bed in the morning and leaving for work the same time every day are just some examples of automatic behaviors carried out every day with little to no conscious thought.

Many habits, such as daily exercise or cleaning up clutter, serve us extremely well in our day-to-day life. However, we also have habits – habits that we aren't even aware of – that stop us from living the fulfilling and amazing life that we want.

Dopamine is a neurotransmitter that helps control the brain's reward and pleasure centers. It influences memory, desire, decision making and is stimulated by learning. To break a cycle of bad habits you need to reset your dopamine cycles by giving yourself other rewards. As you disable old pathways of bad habits, you need to start new ones with new rewards. They may include: buying yourself a special item, treating yourself to something (manicure, fishing, movie, etc.) or just make the reward stimulating or challenging. Pick something that is not destructive and is affordable to your budget. This way without spending a lot of money you have something to look forward to. By doing this your brain will set new pathways for good, healthy, and long lasting behaviors.

When I was a child I enjoyed playing with my Lionel train set. I had the engine go around an oval pulling a few other cars. One day I wanted to make a change and added a switch to create a new path for the train to follow. I added curves, inclines, lights, and became really creative with my new tracks. Sometimes the train fell off the track and I learned to reduce the speed. I found I had to make changes to allow the engine to pull all the cars. Once I perfected this new pattern I did not want to go back to the old one. I often think of this childhood memory when I change a habit because I know that change is good and something better is ahead. The reward for changing my train track was it provided me new challenges, creativity, and hours of pleasure. A reward for you to change the track of a bad habit might be better health, more money, or improved relationships.

Here are some examples of habits that can stop you from having the life of your dreams:

- Watching TV for three hours every night
- Snacking between meals
- Hitting the snooze button for an hour after your alarm goes off
- Checking email every five minutes

There is nothing inherently wrong with any of the examples I've listed. What I'm pointing to here is *automatic behavior.* Are you *choosing* to watch 3 hours of TV, or is it simply a habit?

Imagine dripping some hot water onto a slightly tilted block of butter. The first drop of hot water runs down the butter towards the floor and creates a groove as it melts the butter. The second drop and third drops follow the same path, and the groove gets deeper. Every drop of water continues to deepen the groove.

This is how our brains function. Each time we repeat an action, the neural pathways involved with that action get stronger. It becomes automatic. Without making a conscious choice to do something different, this automatic behavior simply repeats. Most of life is habitual. You do the same things today that you did yesterday and the day before. In fact, it is estimated that out of every 11,000 signals you receive from your senses, your brain only consciously processes 40.

How many times have you done something without thinking, such as driving your car or cooking a certain meal? I never knew how to type. When I first started using a computer, I only used my right index finger to search and peck. Through repetition I gradually expanded to both hands and additional fingers. I recently realized while writing this book how much my typing skills have developed. I don't have to think about where the keys are anymore. Instead, like magic, my fingers seem to do it all. I am programmed to type a certain way, just like when I drive my car. They are both habits that developed with time and repetition.

I drove my car to work the same way for 16 years. It seemed that after a while the car knew where to go, when to turn and what expressway exit to get off at. I didn't have to look at roadmaps or use GPS. Everything was automatic. It was a habit formed by repetition. Subconsciously I looked for the landmarks and signs while my mind would drift.

One day we moved. I had to work hard to break the habit of getting off the exit I had used for many years. Several times I did not pay attention and actually got off at my old exit. In fact, one day I actually not only got off at the wrong exit again but drove about a mile before I realized it. It took about four weeks to reprogram myself to break this old habit and drive to the new exit without any thought.

Fundamentally, this book is about identifying and changing habits that stop you from having the life of your dreams. The invitation is for you to relate to your actions and behavior in a conscious manner, and to repeatedly practice taking *new* actions that move you forward. The exercises and worksheets in this book are specifically designed to support you in tracking and changing your automatic behaviors.

By taking on the practices in this book, you will no longer be a slave to your habits. You will be able to choose the ones you want to keep and create new ones in place of habits that don't serve you. With every choice you make you create your life. You will make mistakes along the way. You can't run away from your mistakes. You need to fix them as soon as possible. We are all human and we will make mistakes. Just remember, mistakes are proof that you are trying

> *"A life making mistakes is not only more honorable, but more useful than a life spent doing nothing at all."*
>
> \- George Bernard Shaw.

Let me take a moment to distinguish between habits and addictions. A substance addiction is a compulsive need for and use of a habit-forming substance (such as nicotine, alcohol or heroin), characterized by tolerance and by well-defined physiological symptoms upon withdrawal. A process addiction is a persistent, compulsive dependence on a behavior (such as gambling, eating or sexual activity).

Essentially, an addiction is a medical condition. The practices outlined in this book may be helpful for an addict if used in conjunction with professional or medical support, but these practices are not intended as treatment for individual addictions. If you are concerned that you or anyone that you know has an addiction, I strongly recommend visiting your family doctor, or visiting www.addictionresourceguide.

com for a comprehensive directory of all addiction treatment facilities and resources.

Tips and Tricks for Forming Effective Habits:

- **Work on forming one habit at a time for 30 days at a time.** Success is more likely if you focus on frequent repetition of one habit at a time.
- **Use a trigger.** A trigger is a short ritual that leads to the desired behavior. For example, if you want to make flossing your teeth a habit, place the floss directly beside your toothbrush. When you see the floss as you grab your toothbrush, put the toothbrush down and floss first.
- **Replace lost needs.** Consider the need that your habit is filling. For example, are you watching TV for three hours per day because you are bored? Try calling a friend or volunteering to connect with your community.
- **Eliminate bad thoughts.** When you find yourself thinking negatively about your progress, remind yourself about the positive change you are making. (Or try going deeper – is thinking negatively also a habit?)
- **Write it down.** Create clarity by defining what you want your change to be. Print and post your goal. Visual cues help you stay committed.
- **Get support.** Tell several people that you are creating a new habit. Report your progress to a friend each day.
- **Keep it simple.** Your change should involve only one or two rules. Simple rules create success.
- **Be consistent.** The point of a habit is that it is automatic. Repeat the behavior consciously until you don't need to think about it anymore.

Before we move on, I want to be clear about one very important thing: *there is nothing wrong with you.* Everyone has room for self-growth and personal development. There is no better way to break a bad habit than knowing you have the confidence to do it. By reading and using this book you will be able to re-engineer your life and become the person you were meant to be.

Developing new habits isn't about "fixing you" or identifying a whole bunch of places where you are living your life "wrong" so that you can get it "right." All of the exercises in this book assume that you – as you are right now – are fully capable, and *worthy*, of creating what you want in life.

This distinction is important. If you take on the exercises in this book hoping that in the end, you will be a "better person," you might find yourself disappointed. There is no "salvation" on the other side. It's right here, right now, the minute you choose to see and receive it.

There is a huge difference between reading this book while thinking, "I will do all of these things, and THEN I can have the success I want!" and reading this book while thinking, "Success is already available in my life, right here and right now, and I will use the exercises in this book to support me in living into that."

Being successful is like figuring out the numbers in a combination lock. You need all the numbers in the correct order to open it up. Most people probably have some of those numbers, if not all of them already. Now all they have to do is line them up in the right order.

Steve was a school teacher for over 30 years. He contacted me about the next chapter of his life, retirement. As a transition coach, my job is to ask the right questions and have Steve come up with the answers. Steve is basically happily married. His three children are grown up and doing well on their own. His wife retired from the corporate world the year before and has become the full time babysitter for their three year old granddaughter.

There are certain areas in your life that have to be in balance in order to bring joy into your life. They are; health, finance, spirituality, emotions, relationships, and career. These are the numbers to your own personal combination lock. After asking Steve many questions and doing other activities, Steve basically had all the numbers aligned and was happy. His wife really wanted him to retire and do more with her. In his heart he knew it was time to retire. The problem was he was afraid to. Fear of change is a concern for many people. The numbers on his combination lock were about to get juggled around. Where he scored high on career was changing. He always had a good balance with free time, especially as a teacher. Now he was afraid of too much free time. In fact, that could actually put a strain on his relationship with his wife. What would it be like to spend 24/7 with one person? He also knew he would lose the companionship of his friends at school. Fortunately, his health was good, he and his wife would have good pensions, and he was a very spiritual person. Retirement for some people is not the happy time they expect. Too much idle time for anyone can actually lead to boredom and stress.

As a transition coach, I worked with Steve on a weekly basis. He decided to retire and felt good about his decision. His wife did too. Together we planned his goals, dreams, and objectives. I was his cheerleader and throughout this process I was there to help monitor his progress and offer encouragement.

I spoke to him recently and he is "doing great." He made adjustments and once again has a balance in his life. He and his wife enjoy traveling, their family and friends. He has taken up some new activities, including golf and fishing. He works for a friend part time doing some carpentry work. Steve volunteers with his wife at a local charity a few hours each week, giving back to those less fortunate. He has met friends from all his new activities. The best thing is that he can do what he wants, when he wants. All it took was being willing to make some adjustments to this new stage of life.

The big "secret" of this book is that you can be happy and feel great this instant. What I've found though, is that many people's habits are born from and support the notion that there is something wrong with you, and that you don't deserve happiness unless you fix yourself.

For example, one woman I know had a habit of setting huge goals for herself. In her first year of starting a new business – in an area where she had no prior experience – she set a goal of generating over $100,000 in her first year. She said that by month 6, she would bring in $12,000 per month. Most of the people starting out in her field take six months to generate $3,000 per month.

When she didn't meet her goal in month 6, she set an even *higher* goal for month 7. When she didn't meet that goal, she set an *even higher* goal for month 8. In her business, there was no fun, no joy, no play, no room for error, and no chance of success. Her "habit" was to set herself up to fail over and over and over again. Why? Because she didn't believe she deserved happiness. She thought there was something wrong with her, and that by meeting grandiose targets she would somehow be able to prove her worth.

By noticing this habit, and recognizing that in effect she was punishing herself for her perceived "imperfectness," she was able to practice letting go of her impossibly high expectations of herself, and find peace in her life.

Before reading any further, take a deep breath, and say, "There is nothing wrong with me." If you start to relate to the practices and suggestions in this book as conditions for your happiness (i.e. "when

I change this habit, then I can be happy"), STOP, take a deep breath, and say "There is nothing wrong with me."

As you read through the remainder of this book, you will be introduced to exercises and practices that will support you in changing your habits around your well being, your money, your time, and your dreams. The premise of all of these exercises is that you *deserve* happiness. You deserve to treat yourself well, to live an abundant and free life, and to contribute your unique gifts to the world. We are building new pathways that are rooted in the belief that you are perfect the way you are, and that happiness and feeling great are available to you right now.

Remember, it's OK to make mistakes. In fact, I guarantee that you will make them. Expect to falter and plan for setbacks. A slip does not mean failure. The people who are most successful at giving up smoking are the ones who have "quit" 10-12 times. Every time you try a new pathway, it gets stronger – even if you take a walk down memory lane, and visit the old pathway sometimes.

You CAN do this. I believe in you. Let's do this together.

> "Even beach glass requires broken bottles and rough waters to become truly beautiful."
>
> - Melissa Malkush

CHAPTER 2

Living The Responsible Life

"Most people do not really want freedom, because freedom involves responsibility, and most people are frightened of responsibility."

- Sigmund Freud

Before we get started on exciting topics like money and dreams, let's spend some time on the subject of *responsibility*.

Hey, come back here! Don't turn the page. This is a *really* important discussion, and it is the *key* to your success.

What do you think of when you think of "being responsible"? If you are like most people, being responsible means making and fulfilling promises, showing up on time, meeting your obligations, making enough money to pay the bills, staying organized, and taking the blame and accepting the consequences of your own mistakes.

For some of you, this is an obvious picture of responsibility, and you naturally take it on - if not happily, then at least stoically. For others, being responsible seems like a burden – heavy and exhausting – and you want to avoid it at all costs.

In my view, the above description of "responsibility" is incomplete. Consider the following fictional scenario:

Jack is an employee at a large technology company that manufactures software. Jack is tasked with reviewing customer complaints and questions, and relating common concerns to the engineers who create the software. Jack arrives at work on time daily. He listens to customer complaints, and uses the tools available to him to address the customers' issues. On the occasions where customers say they have been misunderstood, Jack follows up with those customers, and offers them an alternative solution to their problems. In two years, Jack is promoted to the position of customer relations manager, supervising a team of people in his old position.

I would like you to play with this scenario in a couple of different ways. First, notice that there are no interpretations about what is "good" or "bad" in this scenario. Every sentence simply relays a piece of neutral information. Read the scenario again to confirm this.

Now, take a minute to notice the interpretation you assigned to this scenario. My instinct is to relate to this scenario as "good" – Jack is a "good" employee, Jack has a "good" work ethic. *I* have assigned value to arriving on time. I assume that Jack was promoted because he was "good" at his job, so *I* have also assigned value to promotion. My interpretation of this scenario is based on *my* experiences, *my* values, and *my* education. There is nothing wrong with my interpretation, but it is exclusively *mine*, and I am responsible for how I relate to this scenario, just as you are responsible for how *you* relate to the scenario. I am also responsible for how I relate to all of the circumstances, events, and people around me. I am responsible for my relationship to time, my interpretation of what my children say to me, and my reaction to the nightly news. I own it. It's mine.

Second, I want you to notice that in this scenario, Jack likely meets all of the criteria in our above description of responsibility (at least, that is *my* interpretation). Does this mean that Jack is responsible?

Maybe but here is the missing piece: freedom. Does Jack feel free in his job, and his life? Is he happy? Is this life what he wants, or is he trapped in a routine that leaves him feeling unfulfilled and dissatisfied?

Here's the thing: we have been told that "with freedom, comes responsibility." Well, I am going to flip that on its head.

From responsibility, comes freedom. Responsibility is a source of freedom. Being responsible – being the source of your own results – is deeply liberating, and immensely satisfying. YOU hold the key to your ALL of your dreams.

Consider the following statements:

- I would love to start my own business, but the economy sucks.
- I'm not getting paid enough for my work.
- My friends always waste my time when they are late.

Who has the power in those situations? The economy, your boss, and your friends! When you say things like that, the implication is that you are completely powerless. There is no freedom or power or satisfaction in placing blame or giving responsibility to others.

YOU are the source of your own life. That is what responsibility means. The *outcome* of being responsible may mean that you keep your promises, arrive on time, and make money. However, there is a big difference between doing these things because you are being power*ful* in your life, and doing these things because you feel power*less*.

You are capable of producing all of the results that you want in your life, regardless of your circumstances. I invite you to begin this practice by taking responsibility for the results that you create using this book. Take ownership of your actions and non-actions, without judgment. This book is designed to allow you to be accountable and honest about your progress, and to imagine and design a life of freedom.

Another huge part of responsibility is the ability to be accountable to yourself and others. This will require honesty on your part. Many people withhold the truth because they fear the consequences. The key here is to relate to honesty as a tool that you can use to empower your life.

Practice relating to your actions without judgment: if you promised to meet a friend for coffee at 8:00, and you arrive at 8:15, simply notice that you did not meet your commitment. Apologize for being late. Accept responsibility by stating what action you did or did not take that resulted in the outcome. For example, "I did not leave my house at the time I needed to. Next time, I will leave 15 minutes earlier or ask to schedule our meeting later in the day." Do not spend time beating yourself up; it diminishes your power as the source of your results. If you make a commitment to a future action, be accountable for those actions too, by telling the truth to yourself and others about whether you followed through.

The truth will set you free.

When you can honestly account for your actions or non-actions, your behavior and your interpretations, you free yourself from the stories about "why you did or didn't do such and such." You free the energy it takes to lie or keep secrets, and you propel your whole life forward.

Here are some practices to get you started. I recommend starting these practices before moving on to the next chapters.

Responsibility Practices:

1. Practice owning *everything*. When you are annoyed with your colleague, own your response as your own interpretation of your colleague's words or actions. When you are stressed about running late, *own* your interpretation about your relationship to time. To put some structure to this practice, try the following exercise.

    Before going to bed each night, list all of the things that are causing you stress, frustration or unease. Be really childish about it. Feel your indignation, righteousness, and anxiety, whatever. Then, let it go. Ask yourself, "How can I own this?" See the examples below.

Blame	Ownership
It's not fair that I had to do the dishes tonight – I did them last night!	I always relate to events as fair or unfair. I'm letting my righteousness rule my life. I can either be right or let it go, and it's my choice.
I'm so overwhelmed! There isn't any time for me to do all of the things I have to do!	I often feel overwhelmed when I take on too many tasks and don't ask for help. Instead of blaming time, I can accept that I created this situation, and take actions to get the support I need.

2. List all of the areas of your life where you allow circumstances or other people to stop you from having what you want. *Typical places to look: job, money, time, romantic relationship, parents.*

3. For each of the areas listed in question 2, consider how your life would shift if you were to take ownership for the results you produced in each of those areas. What would you create if you were the source of your life?

Choose one area you listed in question 1, above. For one week, track your responsibility in that area using the following worksheet. When you have completed one week, choose a new area listed in question 1.

	How did I demonstrate responsibility for this area of my life today?	What did I create by being responsible?	How did I avoid responsibility in this area today?	What practice will I take on tomorrow in service of being responsible?	Did I take on yesterday's practice? Am I willing to be accountable for my answer?
Day 1 e.g. (area: money)	I packed my lunch, and didn't go out with my friends, even though they wanted me to.	I saved $15. If I do this four out of five days, I can save $3,120 this year!	I didn't take an action towards starting my own business, because I'm scared I don't have enough money.	I will book an appointment with my financial planner. I will pack my lunch again.	(No answer for Day 1, check in with Day 1 practice on Day 2)
Day 1					N/A
Day 2					
Day 3					
Day 4					
Day 5					
Day 6					
Day 7					

CHAPTER 3

Well-Being – Taking Care of The Source

You - your body, your mind, and your spirit - are the source of ALL of the results that you will create in your life. Take care of YOU! This chapter will break down four areas of your well-being: sleep, diet, exercise, and environment. At the end of the chapter, I will provide a worksheet that will support your well-being in all four areas.

Bobby was in his mid- fifties when he began suffering from severe joint pain. Was it just the aches and pains of getting older? He thought about the years of physical hard work and his jogging days. The pain got worse and the Ibuprofen did not help much anymore. Finally he went to a doctor who diagnosed it as rheumatoid arthritis (RA).

RA is a chronic disease that affects more than 2 million Americans. It occurs when your immune system mistakenly attacks your own body's tissues. It typically affects the small joints in your hands and feet. In addition, RA can sometimes affect other organs of the body. It is a very painful condition which can lead to substantial loss of functioning and mobility if not adequately treated. There is no cure for it, but treatments can improve symptoms and slow the progress of the disease. Doctors don't know exactly what causes **rheumatoid arthritis,** although a genetic component appears likely.

Bobby's doctor initially prescribed medications with the fewest side effects to reduce inflammation in his joints in order to relieve pain. As his disease progressed, he needed stronger prescriptions. Many of the drugs used to treat rheumatoid arthritis have serious side effects. One medication's side effects include:

Depression, fast heartbeat, frequent or painful urination, itching, pain, redness, or swelling on the skin, muscle stiffness, shortness of breath, stomach discomfort or pain. (www.drugs.com/sfx/enbrel-side-effects.html)

The doctor changed his medication to weekly chemotherapy. This in turn suppressed the formation of white blood cells, which decreased resistance to infection. So now, his immune system was not working as well as it used to and he was getting sick more often.

Bobby was not happy with the way he felt and wondered which was worse the arthritis or the side effects from the meds he was taking. He looked into a national nonprofit educational program that a local hospital offered as part of The Institute for Functional Medicine, www.functionalmedicine.org

They teach practitioners how to assess the patient's fundamental clinical imbalances through careful history review, physical examination, and laboratory testing. The functional medicine practitioner considers multiple factors, including:

- Environmental inputs – The air you breathe and the water you drink, your diet and quality of food, your level of physical exercise, and toxic exposures or traumas.
- Mind-body elements – Psychological, spiritual, and social factors can all have a profound influence on your health. The practitioner will see your health in the context of you as a whole person, not just your physical symptoms.

- Genetic makeup – Individual genes may make you more susceptible to some diseases, your DNA is not an unchanging blueprint for your life. Emerging research shows that your genes may be influenced by everything in your environment, as well as your experiences, attitudes, and beliefs. That means it is possible to change the way genes are activated and expressed.

Through the help he received, Bobby changed his lifestyle. He learned about himself in body, mind, and spirit. Today he is a vegan, totally avoiding meats, dairy, and fish. He goes to the gym and follows an exercise routine specifically for him. Most importantly he is off the harmful medications and feels great; his RA is manageable without side effects and long term damage to his body. Most imbalances of his are restored to optimum function, and others have been substantially improved.

Sleep

Scientists don't yet know the reason that we need sleep, but it is undeniable that all of us do, in fact, *need* sleep. The effects of not getting enough sleep have been well documented: irritability and drowsiness during the day; difficulty concentrating; health problems such as heart disease and stroke; reduced sex drive; depression; premature aging; forgetfulness; weight gain; and impaired judgment.

When you fall asleep, you enter five different stages. In Stage 1, your muscles begin to relax, your heart beats slower, and your body temperature drops. You go in and out of sleep. Stage 2 is light sleep: eye movement stops, the brain waves become slower, and you can be awakened fairly easily. In Stage 3, your blood pressure decreases. Stage 4 is the deepest sleep, and is the hardest to wake up from: you feel groggy and disoriented when woken from this stage. Finally, Stage 5 is the Rapid Eye Movement (REM) phase. During this stage, your muscles are relaxed while your eyes move back and forth rapidly beneath your eyelids. Your heart beats faster, and your breathing is less regular. This is the stage where you dream.

According to the National Commission on Sleep Disorders Research, forty million Americans suffer from chronic sleep disorders, such as insomnia or sleep apnea. The strategies set out in the rest of this chapter assume that you do not have a sleep disorder. If you are concerned that you have a medical condition affecting your sleep, visit your family doctor or visit www.sleepfoundation.org for more resources or information.

Adults need between 7-9 hours of sleep per day. Are you getting enough sleep? Be responsible when answering this question: without judgment, honestly assess the number of hours of sleep you get per day and ask yourself whether you display any of the symptoms above.

If you are not getting enough sleep, this is your opportunity to develop a new *habit* that will support you in creating the life you want. The number one excuse I hear from people when I suggest that they build better habits around sleep is: *"but I don't have enough time to get a good's night sleep!"*

Is that what a responsible person would say? Remember that *you* – not time - are the source of your own results. The way you choose to spend your time – whether awake or asleep – are completely within your own hands. If you are only getting 5 hours of sleep per night, and it seems impossible to bump up to 8 hours per night, consider increasing your sleep time in half hour increments.

Here are some suggestions for building good sleep habits:

- **Establish a "trigger" that sets your body for sleep.** For example, have a warm class of milk or herbal tea (non-caffeinated) an hour before bed, or read for half an hour before turning off your light. Remember, that habit forming is about making new brain pathways. Pick an activity that cues your brain and your body for sleep.
- **Create an environment that is quiet, dark, comfortable and cool.**
- **Sleep on a comfortable mattress and pillows.** You spend EIGHT HOURS of every day sleeping. Invest in a quality mattress!
- **Go to sleep and wake up at the same time each day.**
- **Complete your exercise at least three hours before your bedtime.**
- **Avoid nicotine, caffeine and alcohol during the day.**
- **Only use your bed for sleeping and sex.**
- **Avoid screens (TV, computers, tablets) for an hour before you to go bed.** The light from screens affects your melatonin levels, preventing your body from producing the hormones it needs for a good night's sleep.

DIET

People often associate the word "diet" with weight loss. "Diets" are 2-week cleanses, 6-week programs or 3-month liquid-only meal replacements.

The concept of diet as used here is *life-long dedication to your amazing body*. Consider your diet as a source of energy, joy and power - a tool for creating all of the amazing things you want in your life.

Remember that our brain is like butter; if we repeatedly give the brain the same stimuli, the neural pathways triggered by that stimuli run deeper and deeper. Well, in this case, food is the stimulus! Potato chips are a classic example of how food can affect the brain. Studies have shown that potato chips contains exactly the right combination of sugar, salt and fat to stimulate the addiction centers of the brain. It is incredibly difficult to STOP eating potato chips.

The relationship between food and behavior has now been well-documented. Sugary foods cause insulin spikes that result in hyperactivity, then slumps in energy. Anxiety, depression, and ADD (Attention Deficit Disorder) have been linked to an imbalance of hormones, which, with proper medical direction, can be treated with alterations in diet.

Finally, and of course, our diet affects our weight. For many of us, our weight affects our confidence and our sense of self-worth. Feeling great about the food we put into our bodies has a huge impact on how we show up in the world!

Fresh vegetables and fruits are the basis of a healthy diet. They are low in calories and contain antioxidants, vitamins, minerals, and fiber. Vegetables and fruits should be included in every meal. They also make a great snack. Plant a garden and you will be surprised by how much enjoyment it will provide, plus you'll have the freshest vegetables available. Eat at least five portions of fruits and vegetables every day. Nutrients and antioxidants in vegetables and fruits protect against cancer and disease.

Avoid fruit juices! The fiber in fruit prevents insulin spikes, and fruit juice strips away all of the fiber, leaving only sugar. Drink only water and milk. Also avoid canned fruit with added sugar, fried vegetables, and salads with dressings that contain unhealthy fat.

Healthy carbohydrates digest slowly which helps you stay full for much longer. They also keep insulin levels and blood sugar stable. Whole grain and "100% whole wheat" are the healthiest, but you should also check the other ingredients. Watch out for certain buzzwords that are used in marketing, such as stone-ground, multi-grain, 100% wheat, or bran. They really do not mean that the food is whole grain. Unhealthy carbohydrates such as refined sugar, white flour, and white rice have had the bran, fiber, and nutrients removed during processing. These carbohydrates digest rapidly and cause spikes in energy and blood sugar levels. Grains that are refined such as pastas, cereals, and breads should be avoided. Replace them with healthy choices such as brown rice and whole grain flour.

Healthy fats, including polyunsaturated fats, are important for your heart, brain and cells, as well as your skin, hair and nails. Foods containing omega-3 fatty acids are critical to your diet and improve your mood, prevent memory loss, and reduce cardiovascular disease. Omega-3 fatty acids can be found in cold-water fish, flaxseed, and walnuts. You may want to take fish oil supplements if you don't eat salmon, herring, mackerel, anchovies, or sardines on a regular basis.

Monounsaturated fats are also good choices and found in canola oil, peanut oil, olive oil, and avocados. Reduce or eliminate saturated fats and trans fats found in vegetable shortenings such as Crisco, processed and fried foods such as margarines, cookies, and snack foods. Saturated fats are also found in red meat and whole milk dairy products. Switch from whole milk to 1% and eventually skim milk or even non-dairy milk such as soy, rice, or almond. Use olive oil instead of butter when cooking.

The protein you digest is broken down into amino acids. They are the basic building blocks for growth that help maintain tissues, cells, and organs. Protein can be found in meat, beans and legumes, and vegetables. If you eat meat, your portion only needs to be as large as your palm. Preferred sources of meat are responsibly caught fresh fish, and free range and organic chicken and turkey. Avoid or limit red meat (saturated fats) consumption and meats that have hormones and antibiotics added.

If you don't eat meat, get your protein from lentils, beans, soy-based products such as tofu, nuts, seeds and green vegetables such as kale and spinach.

About 75% of our body is made up of water which helps get rid of waste products and toxins. Water can help cure tiredness, low energy and headaches. Drink eight glasses of water each day. Water also makes you feel full and can help eliminate the desire for junk food snacks. Avoid sugary drinks! High fructose corn syrup sounds healthy but science has shown that it has devastating effects on your body, and is linked to metabolic syndrome, diabetes, obesity and cancer. Did you know that there are about 10 teaspoons of sugar in a 12-ounce soda?

To begin your journey in having a healthy and delicious diet (no, that is not an oxymoron), take baby steps. You have to start where you are. If you have no idea how to cook, find a friend who can support you in learning 2 or 3 staple recipes, and practice cooking those meals once a week. On one grocery trip, don't buy any packaged food that has ingredients that you can't pronounce, and experiment with making a meal with the ingredients that you actually bring home.

The final goal is a well-balanced diet of protein, carbohydrates, fat, fiber, minerals, and vitamins. Changing everything at once usually does not work. Before long you begin to cheat or give up and go back to your old eating habits. If you make changes slowly and with strong commitment, you can change your eating habits and be successful in having a healthy diet sooner than you think. The practices at the end of this chapter are a good place to start.

One of my favorite experts on nutrition is Dr. Andrew Weil, author of "Healthy Aging" and twelve other books. Here are some of his recommendations that I have incorporated into my own diet:

- **Eat less meat.**
- **Eat more fruits and vegetables.**
- **Eat less refined and processed foods.**
- **Eat less fast food or eliminate it all together.**
- **Avoid products made with high fructose corn syrup.**
- **Eat fewer products made with flour.**
- **Drink at least eight glasses of water daily.**
- **Do not eat any product with hydrogenated oil or vegetable shortening.**
- **Avoid fried foods in restaurants.**
- **Eliminate margarine.**
- **Minimize or eliminate polyunsaturated vegetable oils, such as safflower, sunflower, corn, sesame and soy.**
- **Use mono-saturated oils, such as olive and canola.**

Healthy cooking itself is a great hobby and can help relieve stress. You can also cook what you like and know all the ingredients in the food you eat. Cooking with certain healthy herbs and spices can boost your brain. According to Dr. Daniel G. Amen, psychiatrist and eight-time New York Times bestselling author, adding these 10 spices to your diet can improve your brain health. It will also make your food taste better. Cooking creative meals is a great activity, especially with fresh herbs and spices because you can add the perfect amount to satisfy your palate. Try growing some of your own herbs and spices in your garden or on your patio too.

- **Turmeric:** Found in curry, turmeric contains a chemical that has been shown to decrease the plaques in the brain thought to be responsible for Alzheimer's disease.

- **Saffron:** In three studies, a saffron extract was found to be as effective as antidepressant medication in treating people with major depression.
- **Sage:** Sage has very good scientific evidence that it helps boost memory.
- **Cinnamon:** Cinnamon has been shown to help attention and it helps regulate blood sugar, which decreases cravings. Plus, cinnamon is a natural aphrodisiac for men - not that most men need much help in that department.
- **Basil:** This potent antioxidant improves blood flow to the heart and brain and has anti-inflammatory properties that offer protection from Alzheimer's disease.
- **Thyme:** Supplementing the diet with thyme has been shown to increase the amount of DHA " an essential fatty acid" in the brain.
- **Oregano:** Dried oregano has 30 times the brain-healing antioxidant power of raw blueberries, 46 times more than apples, and 56 times as much as strawberries, making it one of the most powerful brain cell protectors on the planet.
- **Garlic:** Garlic promotes better blood flow to the brain and killed brain cancer cells in a 2007 study.
- **Ginger:** Can ginger make you smarter? A study that combined ginger with ginkgo biloba suggests that it does. Ginger root extract may also be helpful in the treatment of Parkinson's disease and migraine headaches.
- **Rosemary:** A recent study reported that rosemary diminishes cognitive decline in people with dementia.

Here are some strategies for not overeating:

- **Put less on your plate.** We tend to eat whatever is on our plate. Use smaller plates for meals.

- **Serve from the stove.** When platters of food are served "family style" we eat more and keep picking from the plate. Getting up from the table and walking to the stove with your smaller plate will help slow down consumption.
- **Eat slower.** It takes about twenty minutes for the "I'm full" message to go from your stomach to your brain. One way to do this is to use a small cocktail fork or a small demitasse spoon.
- **Drink a glass of water before your meals.** Reputable studies all agree that drinking a glass of water before a meal reduces the amount of calories people consume by making you get full faster.
- **Watch yourself eat.** It works. When you see yourself eating you tend to eat less. You are also more mindful of what you eat. Try sitting across from a mirror or installing one near your dinner table.

Exercise

Exercise is often viewed through the same lens as diet: a brutal, but necessary thing that one needs to do to lose weight. Through that lens, it is no wonder that people have a million and one excuses to NOT exercise.

It's time to consider exercise in a different light. Exercise is *a celebration of your body.* Isn't it amazing that your body can *instantaneously* recover from overstepping a curb to prevent you from falling? Isn't it amazing that your heart beats without any conscious thought?

Movement - whether it is dancing, running, walking, yoga, or play - is the most honorable thing that you can do for your amazing being. The positive benefits of exercise include a happier mood, an increased immune system, and sharpened cognitive function.

There are two forms of metabolic activity required by your body: aerobic and anaerobic. Aerobic activity means that your cells are primarily using oxygen to fuel metabolism. Oxygen is your body's preferred source of fuel. We use aerobic metabolism in our resting state, and also during periods of prolonged and low intensity exercise. For example, walking and slow jogging is primarily aerobic. Our heart rate and breathing rate go up as our oxygen needs increase. Because we receive the required amount of oxygen, we can repeat the movement for a prolonged period of time without our muscles fatiguing. Aerobic exercise is critical for a healthy heart.

Anaerobic activity occurs when you are not getting enough oxygen to meet your fueling needs. When this happens, your cells will create energy using different fuel sources that are already within your cells. This leads to a build up of gastric acid in your muscles, which causes you to experience muscle fatigue. Intense exercise, such as sprinting, jumping rope and weight lifting are examples of anaerobic activities. Anaerobic training improves your exercise capacity, tolerance and performance.

Flexibility training is beneficial for avoiding injuries and improving performance. I cannot recommend yoga enough. No matter how flexible you are (or aren't), a regular yoga practice does wonders for strength, flexibility and your mental well-being. Yoga classes are offered everywhere; try out 4 to 5 studios (usually for free) before deciding which style and teacher you like. It can change your life.

No matter what form of exercise you choose, it is important to make it part of your daily routine. This is where most people struggle. There is a burst of motivation and energy (usually on January 1st of any given year), followed by one week of follow-through, then a missed day, and then a rapid deterioration of interest and motivation, finally ending in resignation and defeat.

Remember that habit building requires repetitive action. Five minutes every day for 30 days is more effective than 30 minutes for 5 days followed by sporadic once a month workouts. Set yourself up for a win! Give yourself a small goal, something slightly outside of your usual behavior, but relatively easy to achieve. Meet the targets you've set for yourself, and reward yourself! Congratulations! You have created a new habit. Then, take it to the next level.

The goal setting is where many people struggle. They approach exercise from an all-or-nothing point of view. "Either I work out an hour every day or I never work out!" It's pretty easy to predict which of those two options wins out. Baby steps. There is nothing wrong with where you are right now. Be patient and compassionate with yourself, so you can reward yourself instead of beat yourself up. Remember, you are playing a long-term game: a *lifetime* of celebrating your amazing body!

Here are some practices you can take on in service of your physical fitness and well-being:

- **Assess your Fitness Level.** Get a complete physical before you begin a new exercise routine. Determine with your doctor, personal trainer, or other knowledgeable person the exercises to do and the intensity.
- **Set specific, measurable goals.** Why are you starting your fitness program? Write down your goals and post them in a high visibility spot. Don't make them too difficult at first. They should be realistically achievable. Continue these goals for at least a month and adjust accordingly. Having clear goals lets you gauge your progress.
- **Schedule a time to exercise daily.** Put it in your calendar. Do not make appointments or other activities for this time. Treat it as a date with you – the only person that will be with you everywhere you go!

- **Work physical activity into daily routine.** Physical activity doesn't only happen at the gym. Incorporate movement into normal parts of your day. Bike to work. Get off the bus early and walk an extra five minutes. When you meet your friends for coffee, get your coffee to go and take a fifteen-minute stroll. It all counts!
- **Log your activity.** You will be able to see your progress, and it will motivate you to keep going. Keep it simple. Note the date, time, and what you did as soon as you're done working out. There are some amazing phone apps that make this really easy.
- **Report to someone else after each workout.** Your spouse, workout partner, coworkers, friends, or personal trainer are all good choices. Make it part of your routine that you have to report to other people. Make sure that the other person knows your goal and when you exercised. Be consistent in your reporting. If you miss an appointment, let the person know.
- **Listen to your body.** If you feel pain, shortness of breath, dizziness, or nausea, take a break. You may be pushing yourself too hard.
- **Make it fun.** Choose an activity that you ENJOY! Exercise with a friend.

ENVIRONMENT

The music you listen to has an immediate impact and can influence your mood. People can successfully improve their moods and boost their overall happiness, through the music they choose. Music can also have the opposite effect and make someone sad, angry or agitated. It is different for everyone, and you should be aware of how music affects you. Today more than ever, you have a choice with online sites such as Pandora or Spotify, MP3 digital downloads, and premium radio stations. Choose what makes you feel good and happy. Be mindful of the music you listen to and how it affects your overall mood. Be open-minded and listen to different types of music.

Sometimes you pick music based on how you feel. If you are exercising or driving home from work you will probably listen to something different than if you are reading, having a romantic dinner, or involved in quiet conversation.

My wife was a music teacher and I have been lucky enough to listen to and appreciate all types of music. Different types of music have the power to elevate a person's mood. Listening to the proper music helps relax the nervous system and works on a cellular level. Many studies have been done on this. Most classical music is very empowering and has been found to reduce tension and put a person in a sense of calmness. Baroque music, such as that composed by Bach or Handel, creates an atmosphere of great focus that helps with deep concentration. Some people say that listening to Mozart can actually make you smarter. On the flip side, some country music tends to make people sad. Rap songs have been said to be conducive to violent behaviors and promote angry feelings. Rock music can sometimes make someone feel angry, but for most listeners, the adrenaline rush can actually increase happiness by relieving some built up stress.

There are so many genres to choose from. Open your ears and be open-minded to listening to something out of your normal comfort zone.

Singing, dancing or playing an instrument is also a way to bring you into the present moment. It also helps relax you and make you feel more energized. Next time music is playing, be aware of how it affects your feelings. Find the music choices that work for you and help to enhance your mood.

> *"Music is to the soul what water is to the body."*
>
> - Oliver Wendall Holmes

Your physical environment is a reflection of your inner state of mind. "Clutter" is a confusing disorderly state of collections of "stuff" that you don't need or use that takes time, energy, or space. Clutter can be found in your home, office, or the corridors of the brain. It can be old or new clothes. It can be toys, catalogs, papers, books, and gifts. Or, it can be all of the "to-do" items that float around in your brain, popping up at inopportune times (how many times have you thought about picking up hot sauce while you were working, only to forget to buy it while you were at the grocery store?)

Clutter takes on a life of its own. It can multiply with little effort, and you can feel overwhelmed or controlled by possessions. It causes stress and is one of the main barriers to leading a productive life. Unless you deal with clutter, it can cause pain to you and those you live with.

Clutter can cause you to miss payments and incur late fees. Personal finance expert Suze Orman says, "if you have debt, I'm willing to bet that general clutter is a problem for you too." Some people are afraid to throw things out. They think they might need, fix, or wear the item again, and they do not want to be wasteful. They don't know what to keep and what to throw out, so they save it all. When "someday" comes, they can't find it.

Einstein said, "out of clutter, find simplicity." Take a look around your physical space. Do you feel good or drained by being there? Is your space cozy, neat, organized and welcoming? A de-cluttered environment can work wonders for your peace of mind, productivity and overall quality of life.

Your physical environment is an extension of your mind and will reflect what is going on within you. Being in a space that feels good will go a long way in creating a positive experience of wellness. Although we may hold on to our stuff, what we usually want is order, beauty, and simplicity. Awareness is the precursor to change. Keep checking in with yourself to see if you are living in a way that feels in sync with your overall sense of well-being.

When you are ready to begin the de-cluttering process, follow these simple rules:

- **Focus on one area at a time.** Don't try to be an octopus and try to do eight things at once. Pick one area: your desk, the garage, your closet, or just the top of your dresser.
- **De-clutter for fifteen minutes daily.** It's amazing how much you can do if you do it in small increments each day.
- **Sell, throw out, or donate items.** The rule of thumb is that if you did not wear it or use it in one year, you can throw it out or give it away. If you donate it, you don't have to feel bad about wasting it, and you are helping someone else at the same time.
- **Don't allow things into the house in the first place.** Whether you're beginning to de-clutter or in the middle of doing so, stop bringing in new stuff. Avoid the clutter traps such as yard sale purchases and impulse buying just because an item is on sale.
- **Use the "one in, two out" rule.** Whenever you bring in an item, throw out or give away two other items.
- **Put things away in their proper place.** If they do not have a proper place, organize. Go vertical and add shelves in your garage, attic, or other storage location. Label all bins and boxes.

- **Prioritize each item that you are not sure about keeping.** On a scale of one to ten, how important is an item compared to the uncluttered life you want to be living? Put questionable items in a box, seal the box, and date it for one year in the future. If at the end of the year, the box has remained sealed, donate the entire unopened box to charity.
- **Don't be afraid to make mistakes.** This is not a life-or-death situation. If you get rid of something and later find that you need it, that's okay.
- **Get help.** If the thought of de-cluttering and organizing makes you want to curl up into a ball and hide under the sheets of cardboard you've been saving to make a tree fort, call a professional! Visit www.ocfoundation.org/hoarding/ for resources and information on hoarding and obsessive compulsive symptoms and disorders.

Sometimes it's important to get away from your home or office. Taking a break and having a change of your environment can work wonders. Vacations are great, although many times they require reservations and planning. Sometimes the impromptu getaway for a day or two is all you need.

One day I was feeling overwhelmed and stressed. I had a lot on my plate including a deadline for completing this book. It was a beautiful Tuesday morning in early October and I realized I was not focused and had to get away for the day. I needed a day to myself, a change of scene. I packed my things and decided to drive out to Montauk Point, a beautiful seaport town at the end of Long Island. An hour and a half later, after a nice scenic drive, I was at Gurney's Inn, sitting outside having my morning cup of coffee. The ocean view and the sound of waves crashing were so relaxing. I made a few phone calls from my "new office" and wrote a few emails on my laptop followed by a two mile walk on the beach. I left my cell phone in the car for the rest of the day. Quickly, my stress began to melt away and creative ideas and thoughts prevailed. After my walk I did some writing, and the words flowed nicely.

I paid a daily fee to use the gym and spa. After a nice workout, my reward was to spend some time in the sauna, steam room, and hot tub. In between, a few dips in the in-door, heated salt water pool made me feel like "a million dollars." I continued this special day by reading in a lounge chair and writing for several hours, before my late afternoon commute home.

Try it. Next time you feel stressed and need a break from your job, call in sick and take a mental health day, just for yourself. Do what you want, not what someone else wants you to do. You will be surprised what a change of scene will do for you especially if you have a project to focus on. You can really do so much more without outside distractions. Better yet just take a day off from work and enjoy yourself. You deserve it.

Well-being practices

1. Begin by getting clear on your current well-being habits. Use this evaluation form for one week, then move on to Practices #2 and #3.

	Sunday	Monday	Tuesday	Wednesday	Thursday	Friday	Saturday
Hours of Sleep							
Food Intake (record all meals and snacks)							
Drink Intake (Record all drinks)							

	Sunday	Monday	Tuesday	Wednesday	Thursday	Friday	Saturday
Physical activity (including time spent walking, cleaning, etc.)							
Work environment (rate on a scale of 1–10)							
Home environment (rate on a scale of 1–10)							

2. What did you learn about your well-being habits in Week 1? What habits are no longer serving you? What new habits would you like to create?

3. Choose up to 5 new well-being habits (either from the suggested practices in this chapter or choose your own) that you will take on creating this month. Use the following tracking sheet to support you in taking repetitive actions to create these habits. Reuse this tracking sheet for every new habit you want to create.

Week 1

Action	M	T	W	R	F	S	S
E.g. Eat at least five servings of fruits and vegetables daily							

Note: If you are struggling to be consistent with your goal, consider using the tips in chapter 1 to support you. For example, you could create a trigger for your habit, such as putting a picture of a bowl of fruit on the fridge door. You could also take a smaller step such as eating 3 servings of fruits and vegetables every day instead of 5 servings.

Week 2

Action	M	T	W	R	F	S	S

Week 3

Action	M	T	W	R	F	S	S

Week 4

Action	M	T	W	R	F	S	S

CHAPTER 4
It's All In Your Head

*"You have two choices: to control your mind,
or let your mind control you."*

-Paulo Coelho

In the past few years, I have had an increasing number of conversations about depression and anxiety. The research surrounding mental illness suggests that a regular practice in mindfulness – the conscious awareness and direction of your thoughts – is a powerful tool for reducing stress and increasing happiness.

Mindfulness is a worthwhile practice for everyone, even people who do not suffer from depression or anxiety. It allows us to direct our thoughts away from automatic, destructive messages - "You can't do this! You are a failure!" – and instead focus on the present moment and messages of appreciation - "Right now, I am warm and well-fed. I am finishing this job one task at a time."

The sad truth is that many people never seem to be happy with what they have. Instead of focusing on the abundance and beauty of the present moment, they spend their precious time and energy focusing on what is missing from their lives. These repeating thoughts are automatic brain pathways, and with practice, you can build new pathways and thought patterns for your life.

Try this: Make a list of twenty-five things that you have right now that you are grateful for. Add two or three items to this list each day.

Within one month, you will have a list of more than a hundred things that you appreciate in your life, as it exists *right now*. When you start worrying and stressing, interrupt the thought process by looking at your list. Think deeply about the items on your list, and really *feel* your appreciation for those items right now.

Jim Ryan, author of *Simple Happiness* says, "Everybody wants to feel good. What's your thought when you throw your legs over the side of the bed and stand up in the morning? It could be, Thank God I can get out of bed by myself! What's your thought as you walk down to the bathroom? It could be, Thank God I have indoor plumbing! Stop taking things for granted. If you want to feel good, and we all do, gratitude is the place to start."

Here are some other suggestions for appreciating what you have:

- **Avoid comparisons.** Most people base their satisfaction on comparisons with others. There will always be someone with something newer, bigger, or better than yours.
- **Do volunteer work with the less fortunate.** Spending time working with the homeless, the sick, or other disadvantaged groups is likely to make you appreciate what you have. Volunteer in a third-world country, and you will appreciate what you take for granted: clean drinking water, hot showers, sewage treatment, and food on the table.
- **Spend time with friends and family.** Have dinner, travel, or spend time together talking and laughing. Visualize how your life would be without these people, and appreciate that they are part of your life.
- **Make visual reminders of the good things in your life.** Reflect on your photos, accomplishments, and achievements. They will give you a perspective that will allow you to appreciate your life's path and how far you have come.

- **Watch a movie that has gratitude as a theme.** Films such as the classic *It's a Wonderful Life* (1946) and the more recent *The Pursuit of Happyness* (2006) can help you think about all that you have in your life and be appreciative.

In addition to practicing gratitude, take on practicing optimism. The *Oxford English Dictionary* defines optimism as "having hopefulness and confidence about the future or successful outcome of something; a tendency to take a favorable or hopeful view."

Imagine the following situation:

"I'm really stressed about money. We are barely making ends meet. My spouse and I are picking fights with each other because we are so stressed out."

What are the FACTS in this situation? Let's imagine that we find out that the amount of money being spent in one month was $3,800, and that the amount of money coming in was $4,000. Those are facts. $3,800 out, $4,000 in.

Everything else is an *interpretation*. "I'm stressed about money" might feel like a fact, but the stress is caused by placing a judgment on the amount of money coming in and going out. The judgment is an *interpretation*.

"We barely makes ends meet" is also an interpretation. The FACT is that at the end of the month, $200 is remaining. The judgment is that $200 isn't enough, leading to the *interpretation* of "barely making ends meet." The judgment *could* be, "we have an extra $200 per month that we can use for whatever we want!"

So try this exercise. Think about something that is not going well in your life right now. It could be related to anything – work, relationships, money. Ask yourself: "what are the FACTS" in this situation? Stick ONLY to the facts.

Then ask yourself, what interpretations do I have about these facts? Your interpretations are probably based on negative judgments. Here's the trick, though: no matter what interpretation you choose – positive or negative – *the facts stay the same!* So pick a positive interpretation! *Choose* to be optimistic!

This is not the same thing as lying to yourself or being naïve. Be honest about your FACTS, and then choose to interpret those facts in a way that gives you energy, and keeps you moving forward. For example, if you are $20,000 in debt, be honest with yourself about that. Instead of interpreting this as "I'm failing at life. I'm so bad with money," try something like "I'm really proud of myself for taking responsibility of my debt situation, and I'm looking forward to celebrating when it's all paid off." If you learn to change the way you think, you can change the way you feel. Your outcomes will reflect the way you feel.

Imagine that your brain is a bank. Every day, you make deposits and these deposits become your memory. When it is time to make a withdrawal, you can go to the memory teller to request information.

Think about a project that you are taking on in your life - for example, getting a promotion at work. Go to the memory teller, and withdraw all of the reasons why you will *not* get the promotion. Your brain will reward you with a flood of information and evidence to support the belief that you are inadequate and the promotion is never going to happen. Now, ask your memory teller for all of the reasons why you *will* get that promotion. Your brain will reward you with a flood of information and evidence to support your greatness!

If you are like most people, it was probably easier to collect information about why you would *not* get the promotion. This is because your brain has a ton of practice in telling you why you aren't good enough. Practice asking your brain for positive feedback. Every day, write out three reasons why you will have the success that you want in your projects. Exercise the part of your brain that thinks you are AWESOME!

When you realize that you have the personal power to be optimistic, you can overcome obstacles and achieve whatever you want in life. Be aware of your attitude and feelings. To be optimistic is a choice. Let go of negative thoughts and focus only on positive ones. To do this use affirmations which are a positive, present tense statement declaring that something is true (even when it may presently not be). Through repetition, its main purpose is to replace habitual negative thoughts with positive thinking ultimately bringing a sense of self-empowerment, confidence and inner peace.

Here are some ways to practice being optimistic:

- **Remind yourself that life is short and every minute counts.** Make the best of every situation, and enjoy yourself. Pessimism causes indecision and spending time on things that haven't happened. It prevents you from getting things done.
- **Surround yourself with optimistic people.** Observe others, and you will notice that positive people are more upbeat and fun to be with. Spend more time with positive and upbeat people and less time with negative people.
- **Use positive affirmations.** Write down short statements that help you be optimistic such as, "anything is possible," "I can do it" or "I always have a choice." Post them where you'll see them such as on your computer monitor or refrigerator.
- **Don't dwell on past mistakes.** Everyone has made mistakes. Just because you had disappointments or pain in the past does not mean that the misery has to continue. Set goals and move on, especially if you are unhappy with your life. Use these past bad experiences to help build character and make better choices.

- **Count your blessings for all the good things you have.** Instead of dwelling on the negative, think of all you have and how many people in this world wish they could be in your shoes.
- **Help someone else.** Practice random acts of kindness. Helping others makes them - and you - feel good.

My daughter called me at 6:05pm on a beautiful summer's evening. She had two tickets to see Jimmy Buffett and knowing I always enjoyed seeing him in concert, asked me to go. Someone gave them to her for free five minutes earlier. They were the best seats ($160 each) at Jones Beach, New York. The concert starts at 8pm. I live 1 ½ hours away. My wife has one car and is out of town, my son the other. I am watching my twin four year old grandsons. There was no way I could go. HERE IS THE BEST PART. She drives to Jones Beach, goes to a parking lot tailgate party with hundreds of Parrot Heads, and experienced the excitement of a pre -Buffet Concert. She picked out her favorite couple – mid 40s, happy, drinking frosted drinks, wearing their Margaritaville wardrobes while "Cheeseburger in Paradise" is playing on their car stereo. After striking up a brief conversation and finding out they had nosebleed seats – she gave them her tickets. For me, hearing her story was better than going to see the concert. They don't even know each other's names. All she asked was that they give their tickets to someone else that does not have any tickets. They were so grateful. I am so proud of my daughter. Try doing a random act of kindness and help make someone else, Be Happy and Feel Great!

We didn't come into this world to suffer and be anxious, fearful, stressed, or depressed. Most of us come into this world in a state of joy. Yet how often do you hear people say that they are at their wits end, feel out of control, or are stressed?

Some of the common stressors are health, job, boss, school, family, or finances. The body responds to stressful events by producing more of the hormones adrenaline and cortisol and releasing them into the bloodstream. These hormones speed up the breathing, heart rate, blood pressure, and metabolism. Blood vessels open to let more blood flow to muscles, putting them on alert. Pupils dilate to improve vision, the liver releases some of its stored glucose to increase energy, and sweat is produced to cool the body. Basically, your body is put on red alert, prepared to meet a situation with focus, strength, stamina, and heightened alertness.

When working properly, the stress response enhances your ability to perform well under pressure, but problems are caused if your body is in a chronic state of stress, which is the case for most people.

Stress is directly correlated to both physical and mental illness, including anxiety and depression. Symptoms of anxiety and chronic stress include: panic attacks; feeling constantly under pressure; irritability; moodiness; reduced sex drive; difficulty sleeping or difficulty waking up; and excessive sadness or crying for no reason. If you are experiencing these symptoms, I strongly urge you to seek professional help: a medical doctor, a counselor, or a program or religious leader.

Here are some strategies to follow to alleviate stress:

- **Learn to relax. Relaxation is the opposite of stress.** Build time into your schedule for activities that are calming, fun, and pleasurable: go to the beach, spend time with your pet, hike through the woods, read a good book, exercise, or make time for a hobby.

- **Practice simple breathing exercises and meditation.** Spend ten minutes first thing in the morning simply sitting and listening to your breath, and to the sounds around you. If your thoughts race, that's OK. Simply notice them, and come back to your breath. In. Out.
- **Get enough sleep, eat well, exercise and clear your space.** Remember that entire chapter about your well-being? Take care of yourself! You ARE a priority!
- **Clean your calendar.** Cut out an activity or two, choosing only activities that source your energy. Avoid committing to activities that drain your energy.
- **Practice gratitude and optimism.** Your outlook, attitude, and thoughts influence how you see things.
- **Solve the little problems.** Develop the skills to look at problems calmly, figure out options, and take action to resolve problems that crop up. "Put out the fires" or the small problems before they become larger problems.
- **Avoid substance abuse.** Although alcohol or drugs may lift the stress temporarily, relying on them to cope with stress promotes more stress, because it hinders your ability to bounce back.

It has been proven that owning a dog or cat leads to a happier, healthier life. In the United States, 63 percent of households have at least one pet. Caring for a pet can be expensive but for what the owner spends, he gets back so much more in better health, companionship and increased happiness. There are many other positive health outcomes like reduced rates of depression and lower blood pressure

Pet ownership tends to help people adopt many healthy behaviors. Take the fact that a domesticated pet needs to be fed and let outside. That responsibility gives pet owners purpose and makes them feel needed. This in turn improves their sense of self-worth. It also forces them to get exercise by walking or playing with the animal which boosts their health and happiness. Studies also show that interacting with a pet helps to reduce levels of harmful neurochemicals in the body and raise the good ones. Just talk to other pet lovers and they can give you all the benefits first hand.

A pet is not for everyone. Like having a baby, a pet is a long term responsibility and should be carefully considered, especially if you travel a lot or are not home much. Some people are allergic to dogs or cats and the animal hair and dander can adversely affect the air quality. The type of pet you choose and the limitations of your home or apartment are important considerations. Think about your lifestyle and what type of pet will help make you happy.

Mindfulness Practices:

1. Every night, before you go to bed, list three things in your life that you are grateful for. Really focus on each of these things. Focus deeply on each of these items for one minute each. Breathe them into your body and your mind. When other thoughts try to interfere, notice them, say hi, let them go, and practice returning to the items on your list.

2. Every morning, write out the number one concern facing you that day. Write down all of the details, including your feelings. Then, identify the FACTS. Practice choosing a positive interpretation.

Concern:

FACTS:

Positive interpretation of the FACTS only:

3. Every morning, after you have completed exercise 2, write down something that you want in your life. Then, ask your memory bank for all of the reasons why you can create what you want. Write down all of the evidence supporting your talents, abilities, and strengths. When negative evidence pops up, notice it, say hi, let it go, and practice returning to the positive evidence.

What I want:

Reasons why I can create what I want:

CHAPTER 5

Be Here Now. There Is No Other Place Or Time to Be

"Life is now. There was never a time when your life was not now, nor will there ever be."

– Eckhart Tolle, author *The Power of Now*

The most powerful practice that you can take on in your life is being *exactly* where you are right now. Try it. Notice your eyes scan across this page. Feel the temperature of the space you are in. Listen to the noises that you tuned out as you were reading. Smell the air. Sit in this moment for just a little bit longer.

How long were you able to stay in the present moment before you started planning, worrying, daydreaming, or remembering the past? Most of us spend most of our time thinking about the past and the future, which is humorous, because none of us will ever be anywhere other than right now.

Recall that mindfulness is the practice of being aware of your thoughts and directing your mind. We already discussed that mindfulness is effective for reducing stress and increasing happiness. This is because mindfulness is an exercise in *presence*. Being mindful – being present – allows us to experience life as it is happening, as opposed to how we imagine it might go, or how we interpret that it has gone in the past.

Many people wallow in nostalgia and seem to think that yesterday was better than today. With that mindset, ten years from now, you will wish you could be back in time to today. "Old times" never come back. What does come back – and, in fact, what never left - is this moment.

Worry stems from mismanaged, negative imagination, usually involving fear about the future, and about things you have no control over (like the future, which cannot be controlled because it never arrives!) Think about all of the things that you have worried about in the past. How many of those things are happening right now, in this moment? Probably none, because right now, you are reading this book.

Worrying is a waste of energy. It is a learned behavior, and it can be undone. There are many techniques to control worry. You can shift your focus and attention away from your worry. Learn mental and physical relaxation through techniques such as deep breathing and meditation. My favorite is to write down the worries and tell myself I can worry about them later! By postponing my worries indefinitely – knowing that I can pick them up at any time – I am able to enjoy the moment. When I use this technique, I usually forget the original worries.

Sometimes, people are scared of living in the present moment. Living in the past or the future can be a really effective strategy for ignoring or avoiding fears and unpleasant emotions. Unfortunately, avoiding unpleasant emotion, such as anger or sadness, results in a reduced capacity for experiencing joy and love.

I know a woman who had a habit of living in her future. She was either really excited about her future or worried about it. She ignored her past completely, because it brought up painful memories. The present was a stranger to her. She had no practice at living in the moment.

As a result, her relationship to life was very surface-level. She had a lot of friends, but no access to connection. She had a lot of excitement, but lacked true joy – joy was something that lived outside of her.

She started to practice living in the moment, and at first, it was a scary experience. She got present to her fears and sadness. She cried for the first time in *years*, and she *hated* it. But she also started to experience love and joy on a completely different level. Colors were brighter. Her vision was clearer. She felt like she was seeing the world for the first time. Even with her sadness and fear – in fact, because of her sadness and fear (and joy and love) – she felt *alive*.

Life happens in the present! And it happens whether or not you are present for it. This moment, right now, is your opportunity to experience life, in *all* of its many facets and wonders.

Here are some tips for staying present and not worrying:

- **Notice and be thankful for little things.** Little things can bring happiness. Find beauty around you. Watch the sunrise, or take in the view on your commute to work. Enjoy the blue sky with perfect cloud formations as you look out your window during the day. Put out a bird feeder and birdbath and watch the different birds visiting your backyard throughout the year. Watch the expressions on children's faces, or enjoy the flowers.
- **Be active.** Do things that encourage you to be involved in the moment. Go for a jog and count your steps, walk your dog, or take a nice bike ride. Gardening, participating in sports, and playing an instrument help achieve mindfulness. Get out your fishing pole, and get off the couch. Develop new hobbies.
- **Focus on what you are doing.** Pay attention to your senses: sight, smell, sound, touch, and taste. Be engrossed in what you are doing; be in the now.

- **Do something nice for someone.** It could be as simple as smiling to a stranger, complimenting someone, or letting a car merge ahead of you in traffic. Whether it's donating money or picking up litter, whatever you do that makes you (and the other person) feel good and keeps you in the moment. Spontaneous acts of kindness sometimes produce the greatest rewards.
- **Be thankful for the things you have.** When you wish for things you don't have or wish your life were different, rethink these wishes and show gratitude for what is already part of your life. This will help get you back into the moment. Look at all the good things you have. Make a list of what you are thankful for. You don't want to miss what is right in front of you because you are looking at the past or future. If you are thankful for what you have, you're on your way to happiness.
- **Read *The Power of Now* by Eckhart Tolle.** I can't recommend this book enough.

Living in the moment is also powerful because it allows you to *take action*. Think about all of the times you have avoided taking an action that you know would support you in achieving your goals. What stopped you? Probably fear about how the action would turn out (or not turn out), or an excuse about the reasons why you couldn't do it.

Excuses and fear are based in the past and the future. In this moment, right now, there is only action or non-action. If you want things to change in your life, be willing to take action. Happiness and success are choices. Henry Ford said, "If you think you can or think you can't, you're right." Start using powerful words like can, empower, success, inspire, confident, create, and achieve. Eliminate self-defeating words, sometimes called "poison words," such as I can't, I don't know how, if only, what if, maybe, or but.

Putting things off or postponing actions is known as procrastination. Procrastination is a learned behavior that is reinforced by repeating the action, or in this case, non-action. To control this habit, recognize when you are starting to procrastinate, understand why it occurs, and take steps to manage your time. Leaving an item on your "to do" list for a long period of time, waiting to be in the mood or for the right time to fix a problem, working on unimportant tasks instead of completing the important ones, are all forms of procrastination.

Perfectionists are often procrastinators, because they have a tendency to be hard on themselves and negatively evaluate the outcomes of their own performance. They also fear being evaluated by others and avoid such encounters. They tend to think that they don't have the skills or resources to do something perfectly, so they don't do it at all.

People procrastinate by putting off things that they should be doing now; instead they do something more enjoyable or comfortable. Each person is different, so the reason why someone procrastinates might depend on the individual and the task. One reason might be because the individual is disorganized. Organized people manage because they have to-do lists and schedules with precise due dates.

Another reason people procrastinate is because they find a job unpleasant and try to avoid it. All jobs usually have some unpleasant aspects to them. Get those unpleasant responsibilities over with as soon as possible, so that you can focus on something more enjoyable.

Ironically, the trick to stopping procrastination is to *take action*. Any action. Write a to-do list that includes both "hard" and "easy" tasks. When you're stopped, take an easy action, and let the completion of that action generate momentum for you.

To avoid important activities creates problems in all aspects of life and, more importantly, does not allow you to grow independently and professionally. It is convenient to delay a task for a later day because of fatigue. Before you know it, the deadline creeps up, and panic sets in. Other times "Murphy's law" if something can go wrong, it will - takes over. Experts agree that the following tips can help can help avoid procrastination:

- **Keep a "to-do list.** If you do not write things down, chances are you will forget them. A list is part of being organized and accomplishing more. It should be short and prioritize what is important to do first.
- **Focus on one task at a time.** Trying to do several tasks or projects at the same time often leads to becoming discouraged and increases procrastination.
- **Reward yourself for completing projects.** This can be as simple as a cup of coffee or an ice cream cone. Completing a task is a good goal, and rewards work at all ages.
- **Set goals, both short-term and long term.** If you set goals with deadlines, you will have little time for procrastination. Some people put off beginning a project because they find it overwhelming.
- **Divide a large project into smaller, manageable tasks.** Start with quick, easy jobs first. You'll feel the reward of accomplishment and build your confidence, and perhaps the big project won't be so overwhelming after all. If you find a task unpleasant, try it anyway, and you may find that it's better than you thought. Peer pressure works, so ask someone else to check up on you. Identify the unpleasant consequences of not doing the task.

- **Turn off extra electronic devices.** Use what you need to accomplish your task, such as paper and your computer. This will enable you to achieve more in less time, without distractions. Watching television, playing video games, sending e-mail, searching the Internet, texting, going on Facebook, Twitter, and other social network sites are traps that people use to avoid doing a task. The hour you spent playing video games could have been used to finish that paper or report you're working on. During that hour on the computer, you could have mowed the lawn. Instead of watching TV, you could have done the grocery shopping.

Getting into action is a habit. When you noticed you've stopped, *take any action*, and you will be astounded at how quickly procrastination becomes a thing of the past.

Another problem that keeps people from achieving their dreams is not realizing what will make them happy. Ask yourself, "Is this all there is to life?" Write down whatever you don't like about your current lifestyle. What is missing? What changes would you like to make? What must you do to bring joy and happiness into your life? This is your action plan. Identify *your* dreams, not those of your parents, your employer, or anyone else.

To develop and achieve an action plan, define your goals, dreams, and objectives. Believe that you can achieve them, and visualize yourself having them. Post pictures around your room or office and in your car. Think about what your life will be like once you fulfill them. Determine the actions to take to achieve them. Finally, TAKE THOSE ACTIONS.

This is where a coach can support you in achieving your goals. Life has challenges. Unstable economic conditions, a health crisis, or a failed marriage are factors that can bring on desperation. Other times you may feel stuck in a relationship or career and that few options are available. A professional life coach is an objective consultant who works with clients to help them achieve their goals. There are many types of coaches: success, business, recovery, parenting, singles, personal development, teen, wellness just to name a few. Shop around, and if coaching is right for you, make sure that you feel comfortable with the coach you choose.

> *"The greater danger for most of us lies not in setting our goals too high and falling short; but in setting our aim too low, and achieving our mark"*
>
> ~ Michaelangelo

Presence Practices:

1. Build a meditation practice. Sit in a straight back chair or on the floor or a cushion in a cross-legged comfortable seat. Focus on your breath. Breathe in deeply through your nostrils to the count of four. Hold your breath in your belly to the count of four. Now breathe out and observe the breath effortlessly moving back up your chest, into your throat and back out of your mouth to the count of four.

   When your mind wanders, notice your thoughts, let them go, and practice returning to your breath.

   Some days will be easier than others. It is all allowed. Remember you are building a habit. Start simply. Start with two minutes per day first thing in the morning. You can do anything for two minutes. The next week, try three minutes. Your mind will start to crave this time.

2. Set an alarm on your phone or computer to go off randomly several times throughout the day. When the alarm goes off, check in with yourself. Are you in the past, present or future? Practice coming back to the present by taking two minutes to notice your environment: the sights, the sounds, and the way you feel in your body. Aim to be present for a full two minutes.

3. Set up your alarm for exercise 2 right now.

CHAPTER 6

It's Always (And Never) About The Money

Make more money than you spend.

Oh you want me to say more than that? OK, if you insist, but it actually is that simple! The trick is to have the commitment and discipline to stick to that principle.

Money management – debt reduction, budgeting, saving and investing – is a learned skill. You can create (or automate) the discipline and actions required to have the financial security you desire. It starts with getting really clear on exactly how much money you bring in each month, and exactly how much money you spend each month. Track your spending. Mint.com is a fantastic online resource of tracking every purchase and deposit that you make. It is FREE and also provides a simple budgeting tool that can be linked directly to your debit card.

Once you learn how to manage and save money, teach your children some of these skills and the importance of getting a good job. Norman was my college roommate freshman year. His father was a successful contractor who built custom homes. I remember asking him one day, "Why are you going to college instead of working for your dad and making money?" He told me he worked summers but his dad would not hire him full time, until he had a college degree.

Norman graduated four years later and became a teacher. For his graduation present his father bought him a backhoe. Whenever his dad needed underground trenches dug, he hired his son to do it. Before long other contractors were also hiring him. A few years later he saw the need and started his own successful swimming pool business. Having the backhoe and experience he was able to do the excavating and had a crew help install the pool.

Norman taught for over 30 years and recently retired with a good pension and still operates a successful pool company.

To be happy in life, it helps when your children are happy. Get them away from watching too much television and playing video games. Let them be creative and use their imagination to do some "old fashioned playing." Some of my fondest memories as a child were playing store and also setting up a lemonade stand.

Several years ago I was in Hawaii on the island of Kauai. My wife and I were on the North Shore, driving back from Ke'e Beach. In front of one of the homes were three little blond sisters about 4-8 years old. They were selling avocados for fifty cents each. I could not resist buying a bagful. The girls were adorable and I thought someday I would love to have my grandchildren do something similar. What a great way to teach them about work, money and social interaction.

Last year when my wife and I started our vegetable garden we had our 4 year old twin grandsons help us plant and pick vegetables during the season. They enjoyed it and we ate well, along with our friends and neighbors. It was exciting for them to watch the tiny seeds grow. This year, as of this writing, I am building a small farm stand. My grandsons, Jacob and Tyler, now five years old, are helping to: hold the wood, hammer nails, and paint what will be Jake and Ty's Farm Stand. They are so excited and motivated about the new venture. We have also begun preparing the soil and sowing the seeds for this year's harvest. Soon they will open their business, a self-serve farm stand.

I believe it is important to teach children at an early age the concept of work, the value of money and proper management of it. Unfortunately, only four states: Utah, Missouri, Tennessee, and Virginia require students to take a personal finance course in school, even though money ends up being the most common stressor in America.

Recently my wife and I opened a bank account for our grandchildren. Jake and Ty will make deposits into their college accounts. Crosby, Stills, Nash and Young sang, "Teach Your Children." If you can teach children about money management and proper work ethics you are providing them with a good foundation which in turn makes both you and them feel good. I have read numerous studies stating that young people's self-esteem increases by up to 6 percent when they are introduced to money concepts. David Walsh, PhD. is the author of "Smart Parenting, Smart Kids" and he also states that, "Money skills are a form of intelligence and just like languages and critical thinking, they are best taught when the child's brain is developing."

Here are some basic financial skills to help children go from tyke to tycoon.

- Refundable soda and water bottles are each worth five to ten cents in many states. Children love putting the bottles in self-service machines, listen to it crush, and getting the coins that come out.
- A good way to get a child to save money at an early age is to buy them a piggy bank or some other type of a bank. This is a good way to begin saving. Once a small bank fills up, get them a bigger one. Help by giving them your pocket change too.

- Unfortunately, too many children think money magically comes from a machine or a piece of plastic. Get them to help you pay for an item with cash and let them help count the change. This offers a good opportunity to teach them the value of a dollar.
- Some other suggestions for when they get older are: paying them an allowance for doing household chores and eventually opening an online investment account, such as TD Ameritrade or E*Trade.

The best way to learn is to teach. Not only will your children learn financial skills but you will too!

Einstein said that compound interest was the greatest mathematical discovery of all time. Compound interest is when interest is added to the principal of an investment, so from that moment on, the interest that has been added also earns interest. For an example, let's say you start with a $10,000 investment at 10 percent investment rate and do nothing more. The increased value of that investment over time is impressive. (Interest rates are at an all-time low, but the cyclical nature of the economy suggests that they will rise). Watch what happens to your money.

7 years = $20,000

14 years = $40,000

21 years = $80,000

28 years = $160,000

35 years = $320,000

42 years = $640,000

49 years= $1,280,000—You just became a millionaire!

56 years = $2,560,000

Begin saving money today! You will enjoy the rewards of saving money for years to come. Whether you save on daily purchases, food expenses, or heating bills, every little bit counts. Watch your bank account grow while your stress decreases. You will sleep better and become a happier, more productive person.

The earlier you begin saving, the more money you will make. You can become a millionaire by investing a small amount and doing nothing else. When you save money, you let your money work for you. Isn't it worth reviewing your finances and getting started?

- **Establish a budget.** This is the best way to save money fast. You can instantly see where your income goes. You cannot save money unless you know how much you make and how much you spend. After you have prepared a budget, you can find areas where you can save. Review your expenses. Analyze the entries in your monthly bills. How much do you pay for your utilities, cable, and insurance? Are there ways to cut down? Do you need a land-line and a cell phone? Shop around to see if you can reduce your insurance on your car or home.
- **Do it yourself.** You can save a lot of money on minor repairs, home improvements, and maintenance by doing them yourself. My wife and I mow our own lawn. Our grown children still enjoy riding on the lawn tractor when they are visiting. Most of our neighbors have a weekly lawn service. With the money we save by doing tasks ourselves, we can go out for a nice dinner every weekend.
- **Buy in bulk.** There are several warehouse clubs that make this easy. Make sure to buy what you need and will use. Toilet paper never goes bad and will always get used!

- **Cancel unwanted subscriptions.** Many people get magazines and newspapers they do not read. Most information is now available free online or through your local library. What about your cable subscription? Do you need hundreds of stations?
- **Use your public library.** Why purchase a book or DVD when you can check it out from the library for free? Most libraries have computers with a wide choice of programs, and many offer free or inexpensive courses on computer skills, as well as classes and lectures throughout the year.
- **Avoid bank fees and charges.** Get a free checking account. Don't write checks or use your debit card if you do not have the funds in your account to cover them. Avoid overdraft fees, and have an overdraft protection account.
- **Periodically check your account online.** You can also use online banking alerts to keep track of your balance.
- **Purchase wholesale or sale items.** Outlet stores and centers are popping up around the country, selling top-quality brand name clothes at deep discounts. Take advantage of department store sales, especially at the end of the season. Know your prices to understand if you are getting a sale. Shop online, use networking contacts, or find stores where you can buy at wholesale or below retail prices.
- **Buy certain items used.** You can purchase a low-mileage car that is two or three years old and save about 30 percent off the original sticker price. After detailing, many of these cars can look like they just came out of the showroom. Many other items can be purchased used for a fraction of the original price.
- **Avoid excessive debt.** Credit cards are one of the most expensive debts you can have. If you pay off your balance each month, you avoid the high interest rates.

- **Eat in. Bring your lunch and a thermos of coffee to work.** Fill up a water bottle for the day, or buy your beverages by the case, bringing a bottle or two with you instead of spending four or five times more to purchase it. Eat at home instead of at restaurants. It will probably be a more nutritious meal, and you'll save money.
- **Use less.** Turn down the heat a degree or two, and dress warmer if you get cold. Turn off lights and other appliances when they are not being used. Open windows and use the AC less. Insulate your home better, and use energy-efficient bulbs and appliances.
- **Avoid or cut down on vices.** Think of how much you spend over the course of a year on drugs, alcohol, tobacco, or gambling.

While I absolutely believe that the tips and tricks listed above will be helpful for you in getting control of your money, there is another critical piece to consider, and that is your relationship with your money.

People lose sleep over money, get into arguments over money, and choose (or don't choose) spouses, careers and activities based on money. Some people argue with this point – "I didn't choose my spouse based on money! I based it on love!" That's great, I'm not arguing with that. But I assert that even your choice to decide based on love instead of money is informed by your relationship with money: love is more valuable than money, or as long as we are together, we will be happy because money doesn't make me happy. Even a choice to choose something other than money in some way relates to your judgments and opinions about money.

Money is everywhere, and informs everything, and yet very few people think to question – or, imagine this – *choose* their relationship with money.

Most people relate to money from a place of scarcity: there is never enough, and I need more! I need to work harder, get a raise, stop spending, save for retirement, get out of debt, or better yet – win the lottery! The relationship is one of *fear*. Even people who already have a lot of money often *fear* losing what they have.

Consider this for a minute. If my relationship to money is fear, and money – at least in part - informs all of my decisions, then all of my decisions are at least in part driven by fear. Think about that. *My life is a life of fear.* Feel the despair in that reality.

Think about the job that you didn't take – even though you know you would have *loved* it – because you thought you needed the money. Think about the vacations you missed, or the times you were too distracted by money worries to be present with your children playing in the park.

Imagine what it would be like to be *free* of the pain and suffering around your relationship with money. If your relationship did not need to be a relationship of fear, what relationship would you *choose*? Creativity? Play? Generosity? Trust?

Remember back in chapter 4, where I asked you to practice choosing your interpretation? This is a similar exercise. Your current FACTS around your money don't change just because you change your relationship. If you have $20,000 debt now, that debt will remain regardless if you choose fear or something else. But an empowering relationship to money can make *all* of the difference in how you make decisions going forward. It can make *all* of the difference in your well-being *right now*.

Choosing a new relationship will probably raise all sorts of fears and anxieties for you. You have a *fear* relationship with money *because* you think there is something to be afraid of. Your fear is there to protect you from some imagined threat. What is the threat? More importantly, *if you let go of your fear around money, what do you fear will happen?*

Most people fear that if they stop fearing money, they will no longer make decisions based on being scared of money! If the fear goes away, they might start seeing new possibilities in their life, and they might start making different decisions. And the fear is that if they make different decisions, there won't be any money!

So letting go of the fear of money leads to no money. Yikes! No wonder people hold on to their fear! The only options are to be fearful or to be poor, and most people choose fearful, because poor sounds worse.

I'm going to suggest something *really* radical. Ready? You can have a relationship with money that is *not* based in fear *and* you can have money *because* of that relationship. Think about it. If you had a relationship with money based in creativity or generosity, would you actually let yourself be poor? No. You would still make decisions that ensured your financial needs were taken care of. You might *also* make decisions in support of your dreams or world peace or whatever else is driving you in your life.

Here is an example: you are at work, wondering if you should buy a cup of coffee. From your fear relationship, the answer might have been "no" because you feared you didn't have enough money. From a creativity relationship, the answer might still be "no," but the reason is because you are saving money to start your career as an artist. Or, from a generosity relationship, the answer might be "yes" to a more expensive, ethically sourced cup of coffee, because you want to use your money to support the farmers who provide you with such a delicious treat.

You are not limited to a single, fear-based relationship with money. The following practices are designed to help you relate to money in a new way, without breaking the bank. Start small – practice your new relationship in areas that don't have a lot of significance or consequence. As you start to build trust in your new relationship, you can take it further, or not. The choice is always yours.

Money Practices

1. Answer the following questions:

    (a) How much money do I make every month?

    (b) How much money do I spend every month?

Notice that these two questions ask only for FACTS. Now that you are clear about the facts surrounding your money, choose a relationship with your money.

2. Journal: what would your life look like with your new relationship with money? How would the way that you approached your decisions change? What decisions would you make that you are currently not making? What decisions would you *not* make that you are currently making? Get specific. How would you feel when you woke up? When you looked at your bank account? How would you feel when you received a paycheck or when a new client hired you for your services? How would you talk to your partner about money? Write at least one page.

3. Start practicing your new relationship to money for five minutes of every day. Designate a specific time slot for you to reflect on your day, and consider what decisions you made or can make from your new money relationship. Start small.

CHAPTER 7

Timing Is Everything

"A man who dares waste one hour has not discovered the value of life."

-Charles Darwin

Take a moment to consider all of the things that you have *not* done in your life because you "didn't have time." Most peoples' lists consist of things like "spending more time with my family, taking a two-week honeymoon after my wedding, or not pursuing my passions and staying stuck in my dead-end job."

We *all* have 24 hours in a day. How we use that time should be a matter of focus and choice, but for most people, it is a matter of habit and inattention. Time management is a learned skill. Building this skill allows you to regain control of your time, accomplish more by doing less, and live in the moment.

"Pareto's law" - more commonly known as the 80/20 principle – states that 80 percent of results come from 20 percent of the time and effort one puts into something. In business, this could mean that 80 percent of your profits come from 20 percent of your customers or that 80 percent of your sales come from 20 percent of your products.

In time management, this translates to the idea that 80 percent of your work can be accomplished in 20 percent of your work day, if you are focused and uninterrupted. You should allot *only* ninety-six minutes, which is 20 percent of an eight-hour workday to focus on your high priority projects.

What are the high priority tasks that will contribute to reaching your goals? Start noticing where you avoid doing those tasks, or where you are inefficient in performing them. Usually, avoiding or being inefficient with your high-priority tasks is a strategy for managing fear. The high priority, high impact tasks are scary, such as making a phone call instead of sending an email. Pitching directly to the CEO of an investment company instead of talking to some friends of friends who might know a guy who knows a guy who does this thing.

There is a big difference between "being busy" and "being productive." People who are busy are usually unfocused; their energy and attention is scattered, and ineffective. Some people use the appearance of "busyness" to avoid high-impact activities that actually make a difference in the bottom line. The practices at the end of this chapter are designed to help you get clear on how you spend your time, so you can cut out the "busy," ramp up the productivity, and free up your time.

The key to having more time is doing less. Limit the number of items on your daily "to-do list" and use short deadlines to get them done as soon as possible. Try not to schedule more than two major projects per day. Follow the four "Ds" rule: when a task comes in, either (1) do it (if it takes less than two minutes; (2) defer it to a later time (and schedule when you will do it); (3) delegate it to someone else, or (4) drop it.

The goal is to eliminate unnecessary tasks and inefficiencies. Another way to do this is to set short deadlines. "Parkinson's law" states that work expands to fill the time allotted to its completion. Use it to accomplish more in less time. Shorten schedules and deadlines to force focused attention and prevent procrastination.

Have a goal of when to quit for the day. Otherwise, you get into "staying up late to get it done" or "staying late at the office" mode.

Eventually you have to stay late to get things done because you were sloppy and unfocused with your priorities. Imagine that you have to catch a train or a ride home. This will force you to think of what you are doing, focus on what is important, and finish at a specific time. When you follow this strategy, you will get home earlier and have more time for yourself, your friends, and family.

Think about the last time you felt highly productive, relaxed, in control, and focused on what you were doing. Time slipped by; you felt good that you were making progress toward a meaningful outcome. Accomplishment is a rewarding feeling whether it is mowing the lawn, working out, finishing a research paper, closing a sale, giving a great presentation, or booking a well-deserved vacation. The key is to manage your actions and avoid your distractions. We all have a lot on our plate and usually try to do too much at the same time. Multitasking seems to be the buzzword of the twenty-first century, although many times it is actually counterproductive.

According to a study (Nass, Wagner, & Ophir 2009) at Stanford University, people who regularly use several forms of electronic information at the same time do not pay attention and have poor memory or problems switching from one job to another compared to those who complete one task at a time. By doing less, you might accomplish more than high-tech jugglers.

Here are some helpful ideas you can use to better manage your next major project.

- **Start with the desired end result in mind.** Stephen Covey suggests this in his book *The Seven Habits of Successful People*. This way you have clear objectives and goals to focus on.
- **Have an organized plan.** Ask yourself, "What has to happen for this to get done?"

- **List the required smaller steps and put them in the right sequence.** If it is a big project, find subtasks, or divide it into a series of smaller projects. An example of this is if you want to write a book, write one page every day, and within a year you will have your first novel.
- **Identify potential trouble spots ahead of time.** These may include finances, resources, time constraints, and required skills. Know where to expect the bottlenecks.

Take a minute to consider the similarities between your relationship with time and your relationship with money. For most people, their relationship with time is "there isn't enough." Sound familiar?

You can choose your relationship with time the same way you choose your relationship with money. What do you *want* your relationship with time to be? Let that relationship dictate your decisions and priorities around time. You may find that choosing this new relationship actually supports you reducing inefficiencies and stopping procrastination. For example, if you choose "being present with my family" as your relationship, that may support you in being focused and efficient at work, so that your family time is freed up.

The following practices are designed to assist you in changing your habits and relationship around time.

Time Practices

Complete practices 1 and 2 in the same week.

1. Using the following example as a guide, track all of your time for one week. Make a list of everything that you do each day, and approximately how long it takes. At the end of each day, note whether the activity was *busy, productive, fun* or *mindless.*

Monday

Activity	Time	B/P/F/M
- Get ready for work	6:00-7:00	Productive
- Bus ride to work	7:30-8:00	Mindless
- Check emails	8:00-8:15	Busy*
- Chat with my colleagues	8:15-8:30	Fun
- Check emails	8:30-8:35	Busy
- Check Facebook	8:35-9:00	Mindless (where did my time go?!)
- Activity 1; high priority, low-impact	9:00-9:35	Busy
- Activity 2: high-priority, high-impact	9:35-10:30	Productive
- Check emails	10:30-10:50	Busy
- Coffee break	10:50-11:05	Fun, maybe a bit mindless
- Activity 3: low priority, low-impact	11:05-12:00	Busy

*The way most people check emails is extremely unproductive. Allot yourself two times per day to check and respond to emails, and use the 4 Ds rule to either respond immediately, defer and schedule any required action, delegate a required action, or dropping (or in this case deleting) the email.

Obviously, this is only an example, but my experience from observing people is that this is fairly typical. The person in this example spent four hours at work on Monday morning, but only spent 55 minutes – approximately 25% of his time – on high-impact activities.

2. For one week, at the end of each workday, make a list of the high-impact activities you did *not* do. What activity did you do instead?

What high-impact activity did I not do?	Why didn't I do this activity?	What activity did I do instead?

3. Choose a new relationship to time. Don't worry about getting it wrong; if this relationship doesn't work, you can always choose a new one.

4. After completing the above practices, create a "to-NOT-do" list. Eliminate mindless and busy tasks. Post this list in a prominent area, like next to your computer screen.

5. Practice completing high-impact activities before noon each day. Use your new relationship with time to support you.

CHAPTER 8

Just Between You And Me...

Healthy relationships are critical to your happiness and success. Family and friends support you when you are struggling and celebrate with you when you are thriving. Yet most people – even those in good relationships – are scared to ask for what they need, have not learned to say no, and live in constant fear of somehow injuring the relationship or rocking the boat.

How many times have you stopped yourself from asking for what you want – whether it be from a boss, a lover, or a friend? Most people hold themselves back by not asking for what they want: the things that will bring them happiness, fulfill their goals, or help them achieve success in life. They follow a self-defeating thought process: "They will think I'm stupid," or, my favorite, "What if they say no?"

The trick to asking for what you need and want is to remember the presence practices from Chapter 5. The reason most people do not ask for what they want is because of a fear of what might happen when they ask; they are living in an imagined future. However, if you remember that the only moment you have is *right now*, then when an opportunity arises to ask for something, you have two options: ask or do not ask.

Let's assume you *do* ask. In that moment, the person you asked has three options: say yes, say no, or give a counteroffer of some kind. This is another place where people slip out of the present. Instead of accepting an answer at face value, they make the answer mean something. They give it an interpretation based on the past. "*They said no because of that time I walked by him in the hallway and saw the mustard stain on his shirt,*" or "*I must have done an amazing job!*"

The point is that people avoid asking for what they need and want because of a fear of what will happen, and because they have stories about what it might mean if their request is rejected (or accepted, or counter-offered), and they worry that these fears or stories will be confirmed.

Practice living in the moment, and the fears and stories are irrelevant. The only important thing is the next action. Ask or do not ask. If the answer is yes, what is the next action? If the answer is no, what is the next action? Asking is simple; it just requires practice. Start small. Start by asking for something you don't really care about; the objective is not to get what you want (it is irrelevant), but simply to ask. Practice at home, and at work.

Here is some tips for setting yourself up for a successful ask:

- **Know what you want.** Write it down or make up a list. Have a clear understanding of what you want before you ask for it.
- **Think big. If you are going to ask, make it worthwhile.** People will usually give you less than you want. If you are fundraising and hope to get $500 from a business, ask for $1,000.
- **Qualify the person.** Many times, rejection happens because you ask the wrong people for the wrong things. If you are selling a product or service, determine who the decision maker is and what his needs are before you give your pitch and ask for the sale.
- **Assume that you will get it.** Your confidence will help make the other person say yes.

- **Ask in a positive way and remain positive during your presentation.** If you project enthusiasm and are excited about what you are doing, it can be contagious. The more you get the other person involved, the more that person will want to help.
- **Ask repeatedly; be persistent.** Do not give up. This is one of the most important principles of success.

Another challenge for people in relationships is saying "no." No is one of the simplest yet most difficult words in the English language. It is only one syllable and two letters. It is easy to pronounce and understand, but for some people, it is one of the hardest words to say. They want to say no, but they say yes, because they fear the consequences of saying no.

There are many reasons why people say yes. There is a human desire to help each other and volunteer services. Sometimes people want to be nice, and other times, they do not want to hurt the other person's feelings. They want to help because they have kind hearts and do not want to turn the person away, even when saying yes comes at their own expense. They are afraid of conflict and making the other person angry.

Saying no is one of the biggest favors you can do for yourself and those you love. Saying no indicates that you trust the other person to maintain your relationship even if they are disappointed. It indicates that you value your time and energy. It indicates that you are committed to living a life of freedom instead of a life of avoiding pain.

Practice saying no to at least one thing every day before noon. If you are really ambitious, say no to every request for an entire week. Do not explain why. Simply say no. The results are never as bad as you think they will be. (If you are proposed to during your "no" week, consider making an exception, assuming you actually want to say "yes"!)

Arguing is another challenge that people face in relationships. Arguments are inevitable, unless you are a hermit, but even then, I am willing to bet that you argue with yourself. Verbal arguments produce stress, anger, high blood pressure, increased heart rate, and possibly physical problems such as nausea or sleep-related issues. Many times, an argument does not have a winner or loser. Both parties lose.

Anger is usually triggered by a fear of loss. For example, your spouse might be angry with you for not calling, because he or she was scared that something happened to you. People also fear losing money, security, time, and *control*. The next time you are angry, or arguing with someone who is angry, try asking the person you are arguing with what they need.

Often what is needed is an acknowledgement for how your actions or words made them feel, an apology and/or a promise not to do it again. Repeat back to the person what he or she said was needed. "OK, you need me to apologize. Is there anything else that you need?"

You probably have needs too. For example, you might need to explain yourself, or you might need an apology as well. Start by giving the other person what they need. "I'm really sorry that I scared you. Next time, I promise to call if I'm going to be home late. Is there anything else that you need from me?"

When you apologize, do it *without* qualifications. "I'm sorry." Period.

Not, "I'm sorry, but…" Or, "I'm sorry, here's my explanation of what happened." Just say, "I'm sorry." If saying sorry in this way is difficult for you, then start practicing! Apologies make a *huge* difference in relationships, and you will be happier for learning this skill.

After you apologize, and meet the needs of whomever you are arguing with, then you can express your own needs. Make a clear request to have your needs met. "What I need right now before I can put this behind me is an opportunity to explain myself. Will you please listen to what I have to say?"

New needs may crop up during the conversation. By keeping the conversation focused on needs, your conversation will remain present and future-based, as opposed to stuck in the past. Look at your arguments as opportunities to connect with the person you are talking to, by clearly understanding and expressing needs and concerns.

Arguing well is a skill. Here are some rules for arguments that I recommend you adopt:

- **Don't argue when you are mad or angry.**
- **Do not argue if you or any other party is under the influence of drugs or alcohol.**
- **Do not perform or even threaten physical violence.** Kicking, hitting, throwing things, or slamming doors, is not allowed.
- **Tell the truth.**
- **Respect the other person and refrain from personal attacks and name-calling.** This will inflame the other person and intensify the argument.
- **Focus on the issue.** Actively listen to each other, and don't bring in the past or anything else you can think of to hurt the other person.

Relationship Practices

1. Practice saying no to three requests per day.

2. Every day at lunch, identify a need that you have. Practice making clear requests to get that need met. The practice here is not to get the need met, the practice is to *ask*. Practice being very specific about your request, so that the other person knows *exactly* how they can meet that need.

3. Practice apologizing. If you are not in a conflict right now, imagine a previous conflict that you still feel some guilt or anger about. Imagine going back to that situation and apologizing. Say, "I'm sorry" out loud. Say it until the apology feels sincere. If you are resisting apologizing, then this exercise is especially for you.

CHAPTER 9

Are We There Yet?

I have some bad news for you. All of these new habits that you are developing right now will eventually be old habits. They will be unconscious behaviors, they will be comfortable, and they will keep you from growing. If you truly want to grow in your personal and professional life, then you are going to need to get really comfortable with being uncomfortable.

Stepping outside of your comfort zone is the *only* way for you to produce results that are outside of what you have already produced. The new business you want to start, the promotion you want, going back to school and getting a new degree, the trip you have wanted to take for years…each of those things will require you to do something outside of what is "normal" in your life.

Some of the things you imagine for your future seem "easy" – you could continue more or less on the same path you are on right now, with minimal changes to your habits and behavior, and achieve those results. Great, keep going!

Some futures, though, seem impossible. For example, you want to live in the Mediterranean for six months of the year, earning your living off your art, and spending your free time dancing and spending time with your family. In order to do that, you would have to quit your job (with steady income and health benefits), move out of the country, and explain your "crazy" actions to your family and friends.

You will need to take actions that you have *never* before taken, leap into the unknown, and then…

Then you don't even know! That's why it's so scary! What will happen if you do something you have *never* done? What will happen if you take this leap when you can't even see the other side? Is there another side? What if you leap and fall forever?

The "leap" is where your dreams – those burning desires that you have suppressed and rationalized away or harbored with secret hopes of "one day" – live. You will not get there doing the same things that you have been doing all of your life.

If you don't want to get out of bed in the morning, constantly complain about your boss or job, and can't concentrate at work, you could be one of millions of Americans who need to consider a career change. If you are feeling "burned out" in what you do, it is time to do some soul searching and ask yourself, "What do I really want to do with the rest of my life?" Step out of your comfort zone, and *really* let yourself dream it.

Missy is 29 years old. She had a great job in the medical field making a good salary with benefits. The majority of her patients were elderly diabetics and the other employees in her company were mostly middle aged men. She was single, bored and realized her life was out of balance. Even though she had saved quite a bit of money and had no debt she was bored with her job, something was missing. When she got certified as a prosthetist her dream was to help young veterans returning home. Such opportunities on Long Island or nearby New York City did not seem to exist.

One day one of her friends informed her that she was tired of the corporate world and New York City. Sarah was quitting her job in advertising and moving out to Los Angeles, California. Missy helped her move out of her Manhattan apartment, but not before taking her winetasting in Long Island Wine Country. They had a great time and in fact the manager at one of Missy's favorite wineries offered her a job to work in the tasting room. She was flattered knowing it was probably the line he used over and over each day. However, it did get her to fantasize about someday leaving her position and finding another job with a different company.

One day, she heard from another good friend Erin, who also quit her corporate job and the New York rat race to move to San Diego, California. A few months later, Missy decided to fly out and visit Erin for an extended weekend. Erin was working in a wine bar and gourmet food store right on the ocean. She enjoyed the social atmosphere and the fact that her new job was stress free. She was so happy and having fun! She shared a beautiful house with three other people in a beautiful beach community. Missy saw opportunity in southern California. She did some preliminary networking and San Diego also had a Naval Hospital, where many young vets returned stateside from oversea deployments. Missy's other interest was working with a non-profit organization. Wounded Warrior and many other great non-profits are based out of this area.

Missy went home and did some soul searching. Working in her same mundane job reinforced that life is too short to keep doing something you don't enjoy. Unfortunately too many people are stuck, miserable and unhappy with their careers. Change is good except it means getting out of your comfort zone. A well thought out career or lifestyle change is possible if you carefully think about and write out the risks (cons) and rewards (pros). Don't just do something on impulse and later regret it. Missy read the signs and followed her gut.

Ironically she was offered a part time job as a server at the winery tasting room she had visited a few months earlier. She decided to take the weekend position. The other employees were all about her age and she was meeting so many other interesting people. Missy is very personable and the social atmosphere of the winery was great for networking. In fact, one couple that came in was from San Diego. When she mentioned her recent trip to California they mentioned they were good friends with a winery owner just outside of San Diego. If she ever decided to move out there they would put in a good word for her. Too many things seemed to be falling into place. When her friend Erin contacted her to say one of her roommates was moving out and wanted to know if she was interested, it was like a dream come true. Missy had been spending much of her free time thinking about the next chapter of her life. There were many job possibilities and opportunities in southern California. She believes that things happen for a reason and you have to take advantage of the opportunity that comes your way. She decided to give her boss notice and happily left her full time job.

It reminded me of when I was 31 years old and I left my first tenured teaching position to pursue my business interests. It was one of the best decisions I made in my life. I support my daughter Missy and her decision to purchase her one way ticket to San Diego. Life is too short. "Be Happy and Feel Great" in everything you do.

If you had all the money in the world, what would you be doing? Brainstorm this idea, and make a list of all the things you want to do with your precious time on this earth. Your first few answers might be something like take an exotic vacation, buy a big fancy house, or get a sports car. If you think beyond these luxuries, you will likely start considering some type of new career or business or vocation.

You are never too old, too poor, too cash-strapped, or too tied down to create the change you want in your life. Think of the process as "learning" – every time you step outside your comfort zone you are learning new skills and new habits that you take with you for the rest of your life. Life resembles a book with chapters, and we are always turning the page, seeking new challenges and experiences. Personal growth takes place along the way through learning. As long as we continue to learn, we can make the necessary changes and reinvent ourselves along the way. Make a visual display of your ideal life.

Life is a journey of transformation and learning. Dave was 'low man on the totem pole.' In other words, he had the least amount of seniority out of the five technology teachers in his department. He was an excellent teacher, highly motivated, very knowledgeable and the students and staff loved him. Unfortunately, with only five years of teaching experience, the possibility of being excessed came up each year. His job was always saved, sometimes at the last minute, by offering various splits between different high school and middle school classes.

One day, Dave saw an opportunity. The district was considering offering a new MST (math, science, technology) class, called "Project Lead the Way." To develop and teach this class would require a lot of work including; meetings, planning, student recruitment, going back to school, getting a special certification, and learning new computer programs. He knew it would be a major commitment and he would have to leave his family for a few weeks over the summer and take classes at RIT, Rochester Institute of Technology, in upstate New York.

Dave decided he was ready for the challenge. He recruited dozens of students to enroll for the new class for the following September. He flew up to Rochester over the summer and took some very technical classes at RIT. He came back to his new classroom over the summer and helped set up the new computer lab. The first year it was a tremendous amount of work for Dave, teaching this new class and the learning curves involved with the new technology. He had to go back to Rochester the next two summers to take additional classes.

Today Dave has one of the best high school engineering programs on Long Island. He teaches both introductory and advanced classes. There have since been two other teachers from his district that have been certified to teach this program. By taking the initiative and working hard Dave has job security and does not have to worry about being excessed anymore. Dave took action and today is enjoying the rewards of having a very popular, successful, and prestigious program.

According to an old Chinese proverb, "learning is a treasure that will follow its owner everywhere." Develop a new skill, interest or hobby. Learn to fish, become a gourmet cook, take a yoga or meditation class, play an instrument, or study a different language. Step outside of your comfort zone every single day.

This is where hiring a coach can make a huge difference. A coach will help you distinguish your typical patterns and behaviors, and they will work with you to step outside of your comfort zone. A coach will support you, push you, hold you accountable and believe in you. A coach will see your "blind spots" - helping you to identify habits you didn't even know you had. Working with a coach will accelerate your growth and bring you the results you want.

Life is too short to be stuck with something you hate. As Gandhi said, "Live as if you were to die tomorrow. Learn as if you were to live forever."

Comfort Zone Practices

1. Every day at lunch, ask yourself, what is one action I could take today that would scare me? Take that action. The practice is not focused on achieving a certain result; the practice is taking the action.

2. Create a visual display of your dream life. Post it somewhere prominent.

3. Write a list of all of the uncomfortable and scary things that you would need to do to have your dream life. Visualize yourself doing those scary things.

4. Hire a coach.

CHAPTER 10

Follow Your Dreams

*"Go confidently in the direction of your dreams.
Live the life you have imagined."*

- Henry David Thoreau

America was founded on hard work and dreams, from the early settlers to the immigrants over the past century. Bernard was 11 years old. His dad, William, like so many other immigrants in the 1930s, had left a year earlier to go to America to make a better life for his family. The practice of one member of a family going to America first and then saving money to bring the others over was common. It was now time for Bernard, his mother and older brother to join William. As the family went through paperwork and physical examinations in Poland, it was determined that his brother had smallpox. Bernard's mother decided to stay back with her oldest boy until he got better. She had to make a quick decision and painfully decided to separate the family once more and give Bernard the opportunity for a better life in the United States. She would join him and reunite the family as soon as her other son's health got better.

Eleven year old Bernard was scared and with tears rolling down his face, he continued to board the steamship with almost 2,000 other people. His steerage ticket herded him like cattle, down to one of the lower decks. The conditions there were very crowded dismal, dark, unsanitary and foul-smelling. This was to be his new home for the next 10 days.

The trip eventually got better after the ship passed the Statue of Liberty and Bernard went through Ellis Island. After immigration, his father was there to greet him and bring him to his new home in Brooklyn. Bernard started school, where he eventually learned English. He got his first job at the age of twelve delivering papers. His dad, who worked 60 to 70 hours a week as a cook, informed him one day that his brother had died and his mother was not coming to America. World War II was breaking out in Europe and immigration laws had changed. His father re-married and his new step mother was now raising him. Bernard worked very hard and had many jobs throughout high school, especially after his father had a heart attack and died when Bernard was barely sixteen years old. He married his wife, Helen when he was only 20 years old and they had a good life for 62 years.

So many people today blame their problems on their childhood, their parents and use the excuse that they are a product of a dysfunctional family. Bernard took responsibility for his life, without excuses or blame. He could have easily sabotaged his success by focusing on his past and feeling sorry for himself. Instead he worked hard, appreciated what he had and had good values. He lived a good life, and his family and church were important. He always lived within his means and managed to take his family on a vacation every summer. He worked overtime or got a part time job if he needed more money. When he died at eighty two, he was still working at his part time job. Bernard overcame adversity and by following his dreams became his own personal success story. I know because Bernard Malkush was my father.

It is never too late to follow your dreams. We can all achieve our dreams and be who we were meant to be. The only time is now. The only person is you.

Creating your own vision board is considered a key to your success. It is used to help clarify, concentrate and focus on a specific life goal. A vision board is a collage of photos and phrases, mounted on a poster board that identifies a major goal and gives it clarity. It can also be made on your computer and set up as a screen saver. No matter what may happen during the day, a vision board is a constant reminder of where you want to be or how to feel. Making a vision board is a wonderful way to clarify desires and turn them into achievable goals.

Speaking of you, let's spend some time discussing your relationship with yourself. You have to love yourself before you can reach your full potential. Learning how to love one's self starts with making a conscious decision for change, healing, and growth. Stop telling yourself all of the reasons why you don't' deserve what you want.

This goes right back to chapter one: *there is nothing wrong with you*. You do not need to meet certain "conditions" or "become perfect" before you can be happy, or before you can allow yourself to take actions that you really want to take. You can love yourself right now, in *this* moment.

The most important relationship you will have is the one with yourself. Loving yourself might seem unnatural; it may seem selfish or wrong, or you might fear that if you accept and love yourself for who you are, then you will stop growing. That is not true.

Imagine for a second that someone told you that he or she was responsible for your future. All of your happiness was in that person's hands. How would you treat that person? Like GOLD! You would honor and protect and love that person. You would encourage and support them and feed them good food and make sure they were well rested. You would surround that person with friends and family that believed in him or her, and you would sometimes bake cookies for that person "just because."

Surprise! That person is you. YOU are responsible for the outcomes of your life. If you have a good relationship with yourself, you can lead a happy and fulfilled life. Be aware of how you see yourself. Awareness is the first and most powerful step you will need for change. You can't change someone else; you can only change yourself, and the changes you make for yourself can profoundly impact others. The way you see yourself and treat yourself is how others will see and treat you.

Practice seeing yourself as perfect. And if that feels really weird and uncomfortable, practice more. Stop "fixing" yourself. Stop "proving" yourself to others. There isn't anything to prove. You do not need to satisfy other people's expectations of you before you deserve happiness. You do not need to "make up" for perceived failures or mistakes or imperfections. You just have to be you.

If the idea of relating to yourself as perfect seems impossible, consider hiring a therapist or another professional to help you with this. You *deserve* to see yourself as beautiful and loving and lovable; there isn't any reason for you to relate to yourself as broken, and it would be an incredible act of self-love to get support in building a healthy relationship with yourself.

Practice taking your attention off the past. Do not let yesterday make you forget all the happiness you deserve today. Choices and changes can only be made in the present, and these will affect your life now and in the future.

If you want to be happy, lighten up. You don't always have to take yourself so seriously. You have a choice and that should be to have fun and enjoy life. Do you want to be cheerful and joyful, or would you rather be gloomy all the time? If you make a mistake, ask yourself, "Will it really matter a year from now?" Chances are that it won't, so why get so upset? Everybody makes mistakes and with time, problems resolve themselves.

Practice these acts of self-love to make a huge difference in your life:

- **Believe in yourself.** This is especially true if you believe that you are not worthy of love. When you are suffering, you cannot feel love, yet it is always there. There may be experiences from previous years or from childhood that created that false belief. Every person on this planet is worthy of giving and receiving love—that is why we are all here.
- **Write down thoughts that make you happy.** Keep an ongoing list in a notebook or journal, and periodically review it. Changing your thoughts is the key to happiness.
- **Let go of negative thoughts.** Release those that hurt you and thoughts that block feelings that will empower you. If you change your outlook and are more flexible, you change your perspective. Instead of focusing on a problem, focus on the desired outcome.
- **Lead the life you were meant to.** Get rid of the part that is not who you are. Discover the real you. Be yourself, and realize that you do not have to be like everyone else. If you struggle with an inferiority complex, it could be keeping you from living up to your full potential. Understand that your differences make you unique and special, and you will be on your way to higher self-esteem and happiness.
- **See the beauty in the world around you.** When you surround yourself with beauty, you can't help but feel good about yourself and the world around you. Take a walk at the beach, park, or woods, and take time to look closely at flowers, animals, and everything else nature offers. Find a quiet spot to enjoy the morning sunrise or evening sunset. Align yourself with beauty, and it will instill healthy outcomes and a sense of purpose.

Loving yourself is a choice, so make a conscious decision to be happy and more fulfilled. Accept personal responsibility to make your life better. When you love yourself, it becomes contagious. Think inspiring thoughts that let you succeed. It is possible to have the kind of life you want, so expand your positive thoughts and praise yourself for your efforts.

Loving yourself is also the key to achieving your dreams. If you do not love yourself, you will sabotage your efforts, make decisions that take you away from what you want, and deny yourself the freedom to be happy right now. If you do achieve your goals, you will deny yourself the freedom to be happy at that point, too!

Obviously, loving yourself is not the *only* thing that is required to achieve your dreams, but it is a critical first step. Next you need to break it down. You cannot wish to be an astronaut, doctor, professional baseball player, computer programmer, rock star, police detective, teacher, or business owner and expect it to magically happen. There are small goals and larger goals to accomplish along the way.

Start with getting really clear about your goals. Many people have good ideas in their heads, and those ideas just stay in their heads. Keep a journal or notebook and review your dreams often, making sure to write down the goals you will need to meet along your path. Make the commitment to yourself and to your dreams: it will release great power within you.

Next, you need to take actions to support those dreams. Those actions include the practices we have already discussed such as: taking care of yourself, stepping outside of your comfort zone, and relating to your time and money in a new way. Set yourself up for success. Take small, positive steps, and permanent changes will occur, which boosts your confidence and self-esteem. This will build a foundation for success, happiness, and inner peace. Even if you only take one action each day, after a month or two, you will begin to see the positive changes. With time, your goals will become reality, and you will love yourself and the life you are living.

There is a saying, "old age is when regrets take place over dreams," so keep dreaming! Imagine what you want to be or what you want to achieve. Set goals and imagine the end results. Avoid negative people who bring you down. Maintain friendships with people who make you feel good about yourself.

There is no one in this world like you, so don't compare yourself with others. You are a wonderful person and deserve the best. You own your hopes, dreams, fantasies, and successes. As long as you love yourself, you can discard what you don't like and enjoy the people and things that you find happiness with.

The New York Times bestselling author Jack Canfield, and Eric Schmidt, CEO of Google, along with hundreds of other successful people, strongly recommend using a personal coach to help you be successful in your personal and professional life. A coach can help clarify your goals, dreams, and objectives. They can be the objective person who keeps you focused, supports you, guides you, and helps you take action to reach the next level of success. I believe everyone has personal strengths and special talents. Each person makes some bad decisions or mistakes at some point in their lives. The roll of a coach is to bring out and help people discover their greatness, helping them to Be Happy and Feel Great!

> *"Life isn't about waiting for the storm to pass...*
> *It's about learning to dance in the rain."*
>
> -Vivian Green

Love Yourself and Achieve your Dreams

Take on these practices for each of your dreams.

1. Start relating to yourself as perfect. Every day, tell yourself, "There is nothing wrong with me. I am perfect the way I am. I deserve happiness."

2. Set a clear goal. What do you want? By when do you want it?

3. Create a visual display of the timeline for your dream. Fill in all of the milestones that need to be reached in order for your dream to happen. Use the following as an example.

2-week vacation to Hawaii November 3	$500 saved June 31	$1,000 saved July 31	$1,500 saved August 31	$2000 saved September 30	Book time off work; book tickets October 1

4. Determine what actions you need to take to achieve your first milestone.

Example: In order to save $500 by June 31, I will:

- Only buy one latte this week (savings: $20/week; $80 per month)

- *Pack my lunch every day this week (savings: $40/week; $120 per month)*

- *Defer $50 per week from entertainment budget to Hawaii budget ($200)*

- *Post some old furniture to Craigslist for additional income ($100)*

5. Once you reach the first milestone, determine what actions you need to take to the next milestone.

6. For dreams that require you to move outside of your comfort zone, consider hiring a coach to support you.

Make a Vision Board

Create your own vision board. A vision board is a collage of photos and phrases, mounted on a poster board that identifies a major goal and gives it clarity. Materials you will need are some old magazines, scissors, poster board, and glue. Depending on how creative you want to be you can use additional graphic arts supplies and your computer. Making a vision board is a wonderful way to clarify desires and turn them into achievable goals.

Steps

1. Pick a main theme. It may be everything that makes you happy or something specific you may want to accomplish.
2. Cut out or print pictures that correspond to this theme. Use old magazines, photos or the internet.(only use photos that pertain to your theme)
3. Type or write some affirmations that correspond to this theme.
4. Neatly organize and mount the images and text on a poster board. You might want to include your photo in the center, surrounded by things you desire.
5. Hang your board in a visible place where you see it several times each day.
6. Periodically change some of the images or change your theme.

III. CONCLUSION

What I hope you took from this book is a set of tools that can be used throughout your life. The tools are timeless; they change when you do. It takes courage to step outside your comfort zone, but I promise – the life that lies on the other side is worth every step! You are strong enough, resourceful enough and powerful enough to overcome your fears, and take on the actions and behaviors that lead you to your dreams.

Remember, it's OK to make mistakes. It's OK to slip and to doubt and to have fears. At the point where it feels the scariest, that is when you are the closest to the other side! I have every confidence in your ability to have the life you want. If you need or want extra support, find me online at www.behappyfeelgreat.com, and join the community of individuals just like you who are changing their lives one step at a time.

The power to be happy and feel great lies entirely within your own hands. By taking responsibility for your life, a whole new world becomes available to you. By letting go of excuses and circumstances, you create an abundance of possibilities in all areas of your life.

Feeling great is a choice. Being happy is a choice. It's a choice you can make every moment of every day. You made a choice when you picked up this book. Make another choice right now.

Be Happy. Feel Great.
Sincerely,
Michael

About the Author

Michael Malkush has spent his life helping people. As a bestselling author, motivational speaker and transition coach, he helps people achieve their dreams, re-invent themselves and live the life they were meant to live. He currently hosts his own TV show "Be Happy Feel Great."

He is a licensed New York State teacher and spent years mentoring high school seniors with internships and special activities to help them follow their passion.

In his first book, *Nothing Good Comes from a BUT*, he shared his knowledge and experience to help others to stop making excuses and achieve their goals and dreams. It is available on Amazon.

Also check out,

www.NothingGoodComesfromaBUT.com

www.BeHappyFeelGreat.com

Michael on LinkedIn

http://www.linkedin.com/pub/michaelmalkush

If you are interested in Michael's coaching or speaking please contact him at;

MWMalkush@Gmail.com

www.ingramcontent.com/pod-product-compliance
Lightning Source LLC
Chambersburg PA
CBHW071706040426
42446CB00011B/1943